Through the Keyhole

Life, Love and Death Behind Locked Doors

by Steve Jones

For Geoff, still travelling with us and still being read.

After public executions a scandalous divorce case was probably the most popular form of free entertainment in large cities. Crowds would wait hours to be pleasantly 'shocked' and 'outraged' by the goings-on between the sheets in the eighteenth and nineteen centuries. The main witnesses were invariably servants and maids who would peep through the keyhole and gaps in the wall or listen at the door.

The hours raced by as I sat engrossed in the proceedings, some over two hundred years old. What really struck me during research is how little human behaviour has changed. Dating agencies, agony aunts, lonely hearts columns and pornographic works have filled a strong demand for hundreds of years.

'Through the Keyhole' illustrates life from the cradle to the grave; from abortion to suicide, activities mostly carried out behind locked doors. The stories and quotes have been obtained from a wide variety of sources including the country's main libraries, nineteenth century magazines and many, many books long out of print.

Let's take a peek...

First published in 1991 as '**London Through the Keyhole**'
Wicked Publications
222, Highbury Road, Bulwell, Nottingham NG6 9FE
Telephone 0115 9756828

© Steve Jones 1991
Reprinted 1992
Reprinted 1994
Revised (with 16 extra pages) November 1997

This book is copyright. No part of it may be reproduced in any form without permission in writing from the publishers except by a reviewer who wishes to quote brief passages in connection with a review written for inclusion in a newspaper, magazine, radio or television broadcast.

Typeset and printed in Great Britain by:
DESA Ltd.,
Forest Mills, Alfreton Road, Nottingham.

By the same author:

London...the Sinister Side
Wicked London
Capital Punishments
In Darkest London
When the Lights Went Down
Nottingham... the Sinister Side
Manchester...the Sinister Side
(for details see page 104)

This book was previously published as '**London Through the Keyhole**' with the above cover. 16 pages have been added and the title changed to '**Through the Keyhole.**'

CONTENTS

'AT FIRST THE INFANT' 4

Childbirth, abortion, baby-farmers and the problem of unwanted babies, sham births and wet nurses. Child prostitution and the white slave trade. Juliets of the night. Female fashion: patches, padding and petticoats. Male fashion: pretty fellows, periwigs, padded underhose and petticoats!

'AND THEN THE LOVER' 44

Advice for those choosing a wife. Love letters straight from the heart. Sin' in Victorian London. A royal marriage made in heaven and one in hell. Divorce 'from bed, board and mutual cohabitation.' Through the chamber keyhole. Four thousand pages of anonymous sexual memoirs.

'FULL OF STRANGE OATHS' 81

Firkytoodling and flying pasties; a selection of historical slang and bawdy ballads

'THEY HAVE THEIR ENTRANCES AND THEIR EXITS' 85

A visit to the music hall and some of the wackier productions including turtle riding in the australian outback

'ALL THE WORLD'S A STAGE' 88

Nightlife...strange sports and pastimes and life in the workhouse

'LAST SCENE OF ALL' 101

The tragedy of suicide in Victorian times

'AT FIRST THE INFANT'

My Mother groan'd, my Father wept;
Into the dangerous world I leapt

Mrs. Ferry was in despair. Probably for the first time in her life, she had a cab called to her Bethnal Green lodgings. The driver was surprised to be summoned by one of his own class. In 1871 travel by omnibus was the norm, even for heavily pregnant women. The fare to the 'lying in' hospital was five shillings and the cabby would not leave for the City Road until he had been paid. Mrs. Ferry fell to the floor as the driver haggled. It was decided to take a collection on the spot, and as poor people have always looked after their own, seven shillings was raised. The child was born a few minutes later.

Mrs. Ferry's sister went in search of a doctor who at 6.30 p.m. said he would call the following morning! He left her a bottle of medicine. When he did not appear the sister, noting the mother's poor health, went to the surgery a second time only to find the doctor reading a newspaper. He informed her that he could not come until the next day. Mrs. Ferry's daughter was sent the following morning to implore the indifferent doctor to visit her mother:

"Mother is dying." The young girl was almost in tears. "Fiddle de dee. If your mother was put to bed yesterday, it can't be said that she will die today," was the learned man's reply.

Mrs. Ferry died at noon.

This is just one of thousands of cases of indifference to the poor which would have passed unreported, had the case not gone to court. That it should have done so is rather surprising but even though the jury considered the doctor inhuman, no further action was taken.

Because of the awful conditions in the hospitals it was probably safer to give birth at home. Whether Mrs. Ferry wanted her child or not we shall never know. There were many thousands of women every year whose unwanted pregnancy caused them severe problems.

There were three alternatives for the expectant Victorian mother who did not want her child: abortion, abandonment or 'baby-farming', though in the end the result was often the same: murder.

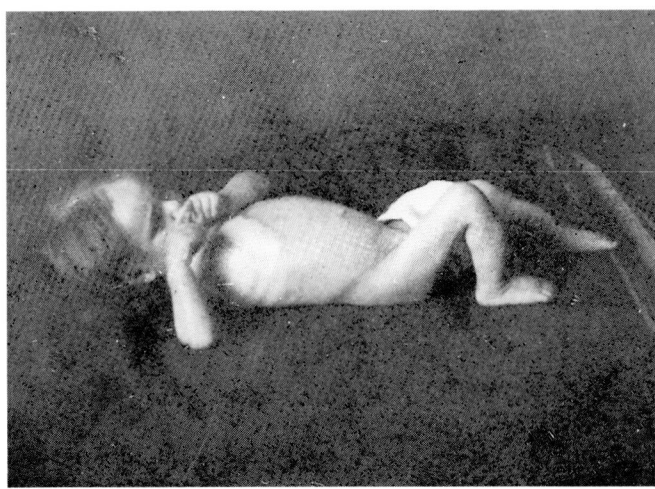

2. Both children are about half their normal weight.

Women from all levels of society might be faced with the problem of an unwanted pregnancy, be they a member of the aristocracy who feared bringing shame and humiliation to herself and family or more likely one of the many servants who would have been thrown out on the streets if her employer was to get wind of her trouble.

There was a maximum penalty of life imprisonment if convicted of abortion though this deterrent sentence was in theory to protect the mother rather than the unborn child. Desperate people take desperate actions and for some women there was just no choice and abortion was a common 'operation' in the second half of the nineteenth century.

We can only guess at some of the methods expectant mothers may have attempted to rid themselves of their child. Most turned to a midwife or knowledgeable woman who made up their own preparations, the desired drugs being more freely available over the counter than is the case today.

High prices were charged and in the top end of the market where anonymity was insisted upon to prevent blackmail, one midwife re-assured her clients that 'the lady's face need not be seen and she should keep it veiled if she liked, and has only to lie on her side.'

The actual operation was carried out for about £50 by a doctor with a catheter and the foetuses were disposed of as premature births.

Those who could not, or would not terminate their pregnancy faced grave problems. Maids would conceal their condition by all possible means and then secretly give birth to their child, some of whom died because of a botched self-delivery. If the infant survived the birth the need for quick action to avoid detection was paramount.

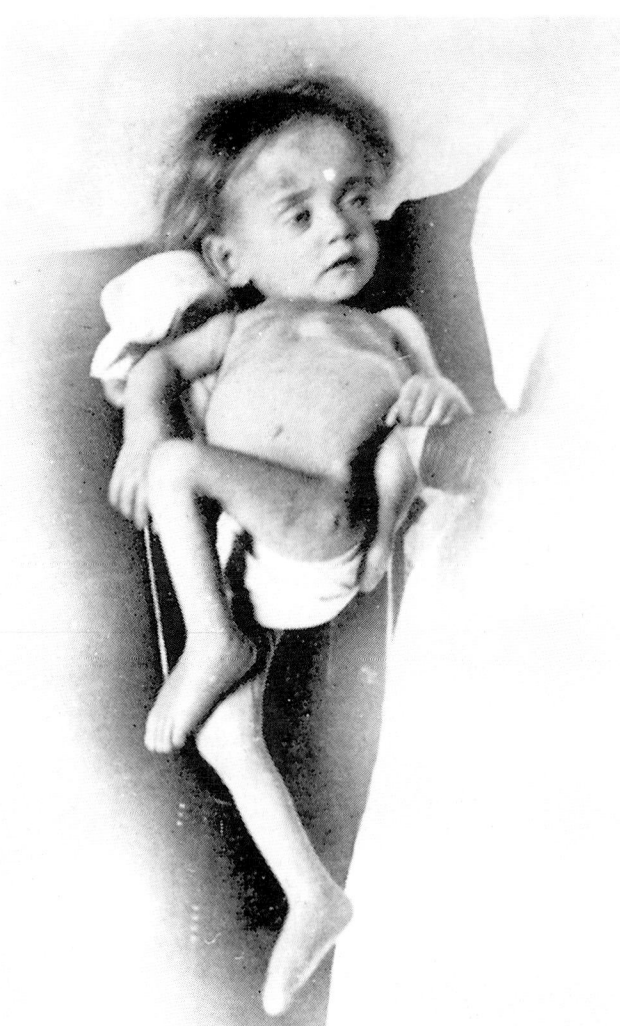

1. Twin children neglected and starved by a baby farmer.

Babies only a few hours old were left inside entrances or on doorsteps in the more fashionable areas of the capital in the vain hope that someone might take pity on them. Others might be drugged so the maid could carry them about without being noticed.

A report in the 'Marylebone Mercury' for Boxing Day 1857, would be typical of the scant coverage received:

> 'a heavily drugged infant was found in a basket by two lads in Regent's Park; alive when discovered but it died soon after . . .'

Some mothers were so desperate not to be detected that they paid scant attention as to where they deposited their children. The Registrar General's report published in the 1860's revealed that:

> "In the last five years within the metropolitan district alone, at least 278 infants were murdered; above 60 were found dead in the Thames or the canals or ponds about London and many more than 100, at all events were found dead under railway arches, on doorsteps, in dustholes, cellars and the like."

It is without doubt that there were very many more deaths than were ever officially recorded. The courts appeared by today's standards to be very lenient with mothers caught literally red-handed. In 1895 Julia Moss secretly gave birth and deposited the live baby in a box which she threw from her window onto a roof. The baby proceeded to wail and when another servant enquired about the noise she was told it was cats. The baby was eventually discovered dead with a fractured skull and the mother sentenced to three months imprisonment.

Other ways used to dispose of unwanted babies are not for the squeamish. The fact that mothers felt obliged to resort to the following methods of terminating the lives of their own offspring testify to the harshness and hypocrisy of life in Victorian times especially for the working woman.

The most common death was due to suffocation, the main reason being that it was hard to prove that, in the crowded conditions, the mothers had not lain on the child. If an examination had been made of the baby, however, it might have shown impediments to the breathing passages, these being blocked up with whatever the mother found convenient: dough, cloth, wood, mud etc.

I am sure that any mother will find the following excuse for the baby suffering from a fractured skull to be almost incredible. When questioned as to how the injury was perpetrated the reply would be that birth had taken place during a regular toilet visit and the baby had just slipped out and fatally injured itself. When bodies were discovered blocking up the plumbing this was usually the excuse given.

The most hardened women might strangle the baby at birth with the umbilical cord or squat over a bucket of water whilst giving birth so that the baby never drew breath, this method having the advantage of looking like a still-birth. Sometimes a trained woman would help the mother and these 'midwives' would puncture various vital organs with a needle so rendering the injury undetectable. The baby might be drowned in a washing-day accident or more commonly just be left to die, both parties claiming it had been born but did not survive more than a few hours.

3. The number of botched births decreased with the certification of Midwives.

4. A happy ending, the children from page 4 a short time later.

Not all women could be cold-blooded enough to murder their own children, and once they saw them, many must have changed their minds. There was no way they could keep them so a very quick solution had to be found. Such is the world in which we live, where there is a demand there is always somebody to supply at the right price; enter the baby-farmers.

These surrogate mothers would take children off the hands of those who found them an embarrassment, sometimes for a weekly sum, but more often than not for a fixed fee with the mother never seeing her child again. They would advertise in newspapers using respectable language though the service was anything but:

> "The care of a Child wanted by a respectable person and her daughter. Having had the charge of children for many years, a mother's care and attention may be relied on. Highest references can be given. Address A. B. Mr. Thompson's fruiter, Church St., Stoke Newington."

Dr. Alfred Wiltshire was a medical officer who, for a short period doubled as an investigative journalist. He went to interview one of the baby farmers and found Charlotte Winsor, not exactly a walking advertisement for the profession as all her own children had died in infancy. She was not strong enough to char, and with her navvy husband in and out of work, had had to resort to looking after other people's offspring. Of the eighteen children she had cared for over the past seventeen years, twelve had died quite young and three had left to go out to work. Of the three she was now caring for, two had scarlet fever and one syphilis. Their mothers were all in service and the fathers a little better off; a banker, a mechanic and an army officer. The women found the payments between 4 shillings and 6 shillings a week very hard to maintain.

Margaret Walters' life had greatly deteriorated since the death of her husband. A Baptist upbringing and education were of little help as the thirty-five year old contemplated life 'in service' or working long hours for precious little pay in a factory. She wanted neither and decided to go into the baby-farming business along with her younger sister, Sarah Ellis.

Margaret set herself up as a sort of baby wholesaler, advertising for babies to be adopted for a fixed sum and then re-farming them for weekly payments. About two weekly was the norm as she would then renege on the deal, not to be seen again. Sometimes she would ask children to look after 'her' charge whilst she went into a shop, never to return, the child being left holding the baby!

The Police, some may argue belatedly, started to take an interest in the baby-farming business (which was not illegal) when sixteen infant bodies were found in the Brixton-Peckham area in twelve months between 1869-70. Because of the high numbers there was a clamour for action whereas previously Mary Ann Baines had commented on police reactions:

> "They think no more of finding the dead body of a child in the street than of picking up a dead cat or dog."

The police started replying to some of the more dubious advertisements in the newspapers and the following insertion on 5th June was followed up:

> "ADOPTION: A good home, with a mother's love and care, is offered to a respectable person, wishing her child to be entirely adopted. Premium £5 which includes everything. Apply, by letter only, to Mrs. Oliver, post office, Goar-place, Brixton."

5. The introduction of powdered milk led to a fall in demand for wet nurses.

6. Some of the very first "street arabs" rescued by Dr. Barnardo.

The Police officer Relf arranged a rendez-vous and was met by Margaret Walters' sister, Sarah Ellis whom he followed back to her Camberwell home. The next day the house was 'raided' and amongst the sparse furnishings in the malodorous habitation five infants lay on a sofa in the kitchen. They were filthy and stinking and had been stupified with drugs. One of these was Ellis's own child. In the back yard another five babies were discovered though not in as bad a condition as those indoors. They were taken to Lambeth workhouse and the four youngest aged between three and five months were to die unidentified; three of the others survived and were later reclaimed by their mother. The two sisters were put on trial for the murder of just one baby, Cowen, who was discovered in the following condition:

> "There was scarcely a bit of flesh on the bones of Miss Cowen's child, and I could recognise it only by the hair. It did not cry at all, being much too weak for that, and was evidently dying. It was scarcely human; I mean that it looked more like a monkey than a child. It was a shadow."

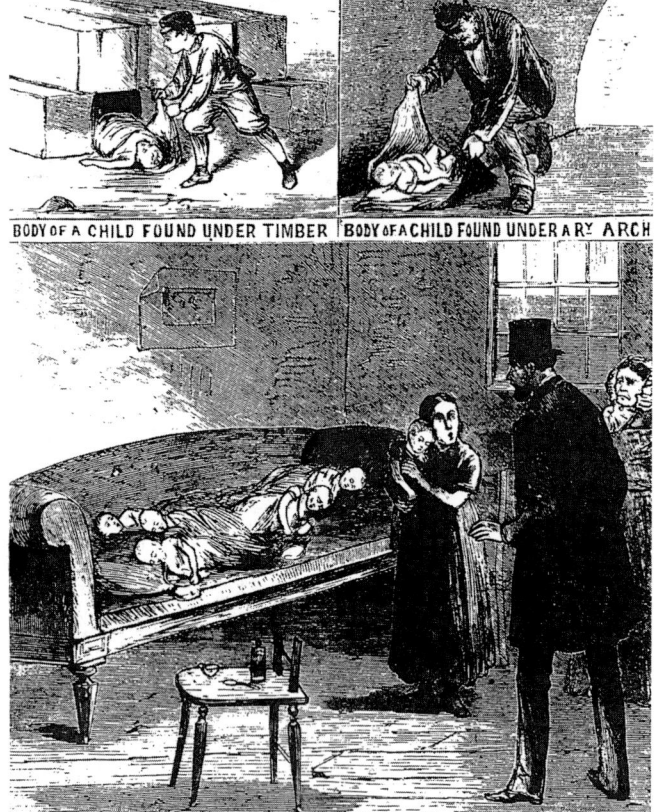

7. Margaret Walters, a scapegoat for the sins of Victorian society.

The trial became known as 'The Brixton Baby Farming Case'. As in so many trials the servant girl was one of the principal sources of information. She claimed to have seen both women go out late at night with infants under their capes and return with just the babies' clothes. They would often hide the charges when prospective customers arrived so they would not be put off.

Margaret determined to take all the blame and when charged at Lambeth Police station she cried out:

> "Believe me whatever my sister has done has been done under my direction; I am the sinner and I must suffer."

And suffer she did, hanging from the gallows on October 11th 1870. Her sister was sentenced to eighteen months hard labour.

Upon the evidence so far presented it seems there is little defence for Margaret Walters' actions. The bodies she disposed of during her nightly sorties had probably died of natural causes and Margaret was only trying to avoid paying burial fees. The baby whose murder she was charged with died some time after she had been taken from the care of the accused and it was proved that a wet-nurse had been sent for to attend the sick child and a good supply of milk had been found on the premises. It appears that Walters had been made a scapegoat for the sins of the society.

SHAM BIRTHS AND WET NURSES

Sometimes, babies were actually in demand, usually to supply a father with an heir, occasionally for complicated legal reasons. An elaborate nine month plan of action had to be worked out with good timing essential. The 'mother' would pad herself over the months — the pregnancy usually taking place when the husband was away for a period of time. She would then move into a room near the date of birth. Once an unwanted baby had been born nearby a parcel was delivered to the room and the mother started screaming and going into 'labour'. The midwife would then arrive with a box of goodies including a drugged baby, stained bedclothes and maybe some bullock's blood and the original afterbirth. After more fake screaming and spraying of blood the couple would emerge from the room, the mother with her new baby, the midwife with £50, both with a secret.

Besides midwives and baby-farmers, a third occupation to be found by poor women was that of wet-nurse. The best and safest food in the last century was breast-milk but some of the richer mothers were reluctant to feed their children in this way lest they lose their figure. They might also have been too weak or died at childbirth and there was a constant market for the wet-nurse though some employees were choosey as to who should take up the role as it was feared that syphilis might be passed on. Others believed that there was bad milk to be had if the wet-nurse was an immoral person.

The Mother's Medical Adviser gave their own definition of the ideal wet nurse in the 1870's:

> 'Her breath should be sweet, and perspiration free from smell; her gums firm and of good colour; teeth fine, white and perfect; she should have an abundance of milk, should have been confined about the same time as the mother of the child to be suckled. Her milk should be white, inodorous, inclining to a sweet taste neither watery nor thick, of moderate consistency, separating into curd over a slow fire. The age of the nurse should be from 20-35; she should be mild and sprightly, good tempered and watchful.'

8. A rare treat, eel and meat pies but no shoes.

9. A group of Barnardo girls. Some blind, others deaf they appear petrified.

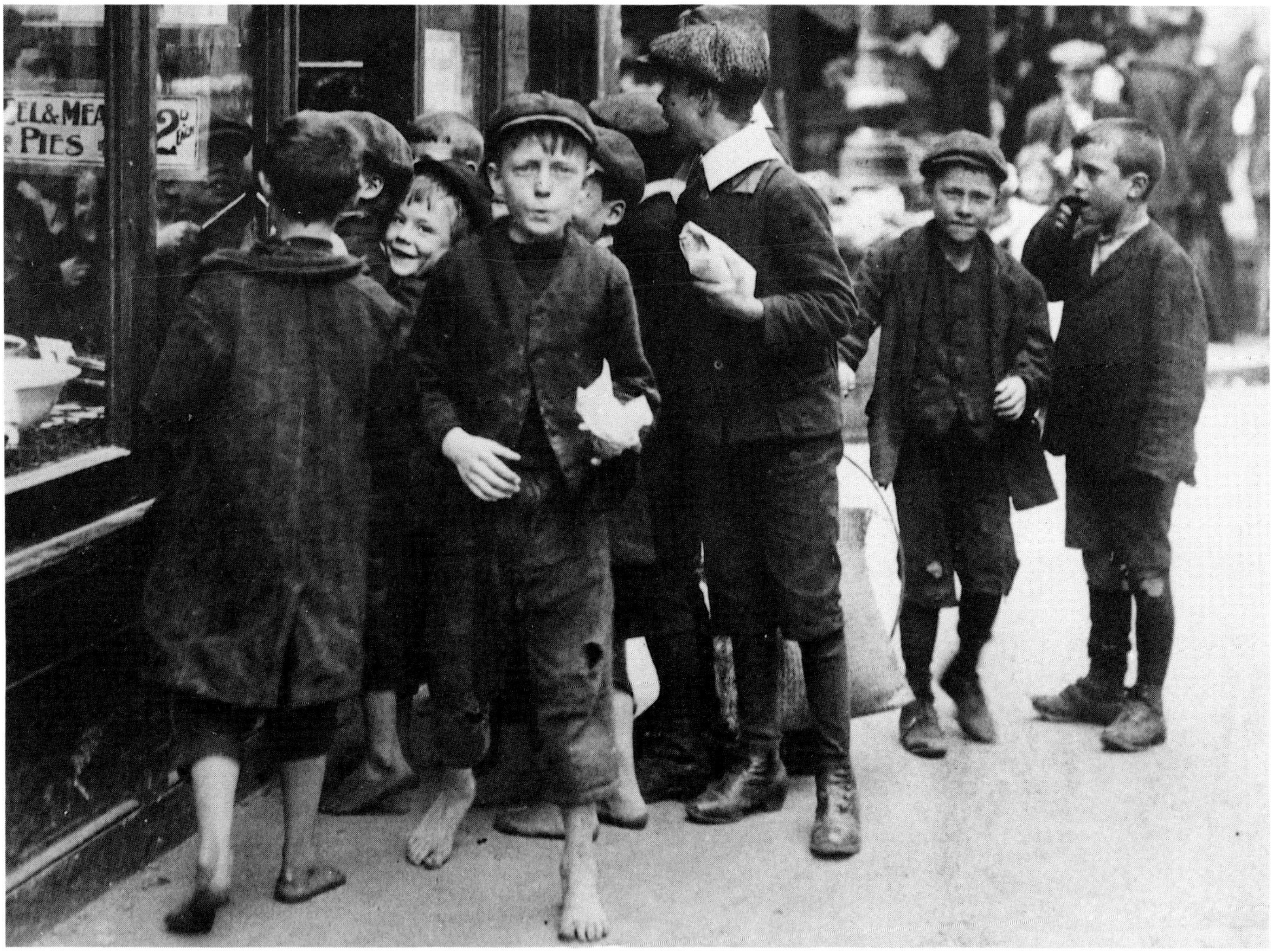
PIES

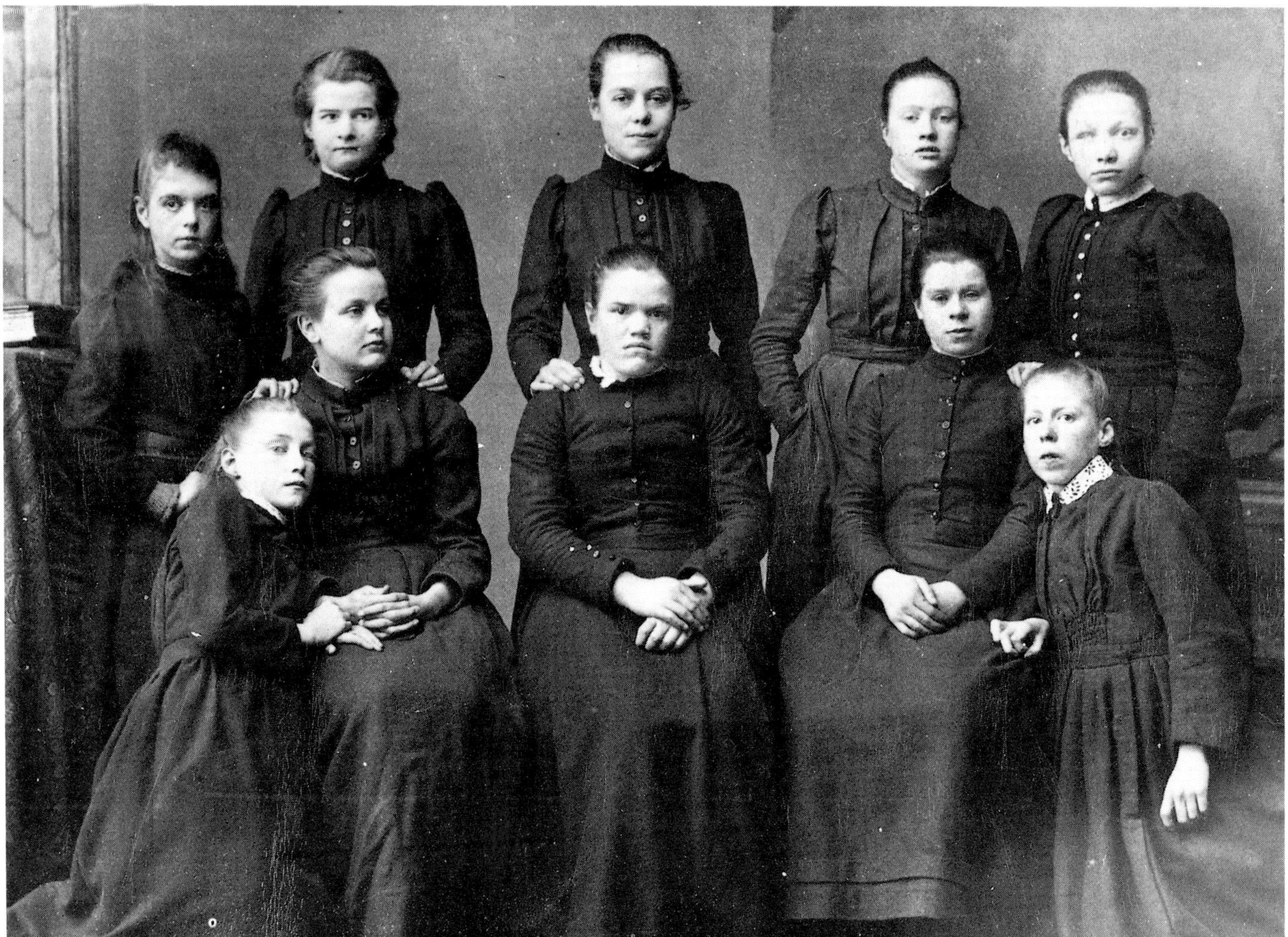

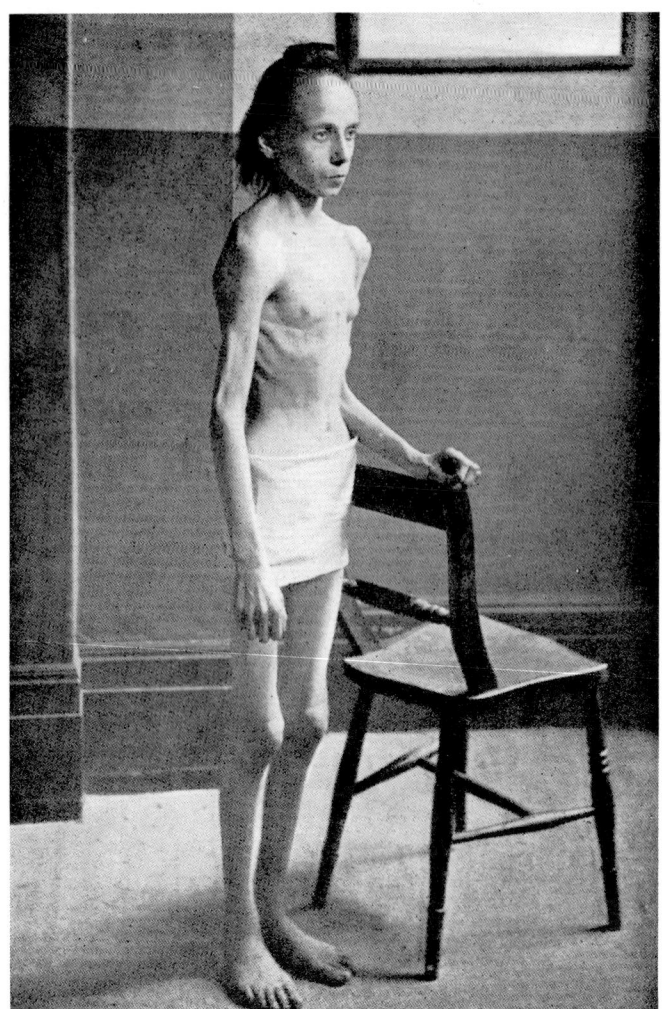

10. Starving daughter of a man earning £2 a week in 1896.

The job was highly attractive as they were treated like a member of the family, with the pick of the food and drink and not too much work so that the milk would be of the best quality. It was rumoured that women would deliberately make themselves pregnant to maintain this high standard of living, but would often neglect their own children. They were not popular members of the household as other servants resented their high wages and easy-life and they could have been a further temptation to the master of the house.

If the babies would not sleep it was not uncommon for the wet-nurse to rub opiates into their nipples to ensure a good night. The demand for these nurses dropped off with the introduction of substitute drinks and baby foods.

Well, if you survived this long what sort of life could you expect?

LOW LODGING-HOUSES AND OVERCROWDING

James Greenwood took an interest in the plight of children in the 1860s and described the conditions that many tens of thousands had to endure. The following extract is from 'The Seven Curses of London.'

> "I have seen grown persons of both sexes sleeping in common with their parents, brothers and sisters, and cousins, and even the casual acquaintance of a day's tramp, occupying the same bed of filthy rags or straw; a woman suffering in travail, in the midst of males and females of different families that tenant the same room, where birth and death go hand in hand; where the child but newly born, the patient cast down with fever, and the corpse waiting for intorment, have no separation from each other, or from the rest of the inmates. Of the many cases to which I have alluded, there are some which have commanded my attention by reason of their unusual depravity — cases in which from three to four adults of both sexes, with many children were lodging in the same room, and often sleeping in the same bed. I have note of three or four localities, where forty-eight men, seventy-three women, and fifty-nine children are living in thirty-four rooms. In one room there are two men, three women and five children, and in another one man, four women, and two children; and when about a fortnight since, I found it occupied by one man, two women, and two children; and it was the dead body of a poor girl who had died in childbirth a few days before. The body was stretched out on the bare floor, without shroud or coffin."

Another contemporary report supported these findings:

> 'The first bed contained the defendant, his wife, a boy of sixteen, and a girl of fourteen, with another boy of ten, and an infant. In the second bed there was a woman, a girl and a child; in the third bed a man, his wife, a girl of sixteen, and two boys (twelve and seven); with a fourth bed, a woman and two boys; and in the fifth a man. There were no partitions of any kind to separate the sexes. The total number of persons in the room was twenty, but seven only were allowed.'

11. The same girl one month later.

254 JOHN   11. Admitted July 26th, 1875.

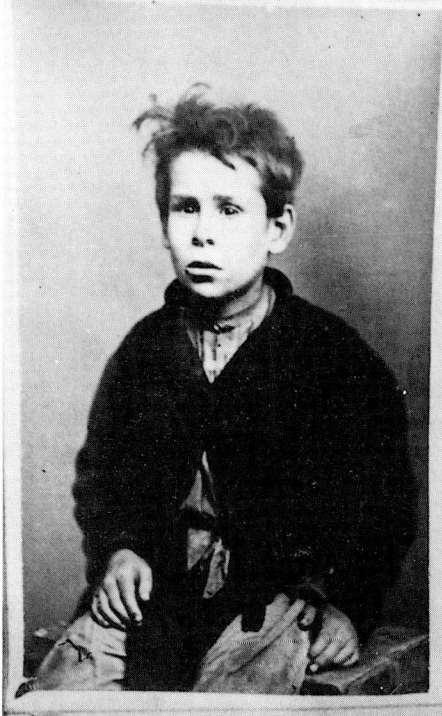

Came here by himself on the above-named date, with the now common story of "I have got no father nor mother and no home."

He last resided with his mother at 27, Albert Street, Shadwell. His mother, he says, is a dressmaker. The reason he came to the Home was because his mother went away for some days, and his mother's landlady told him he had better come here.

His father was a ship carpenter, and has been dead about two years. He died at Rio Janeiro.

He says he has a sister somewhere in America.

The street in which his mother resides bears a very bad name and is the resort of prostitutes, and there are several "Brothels" there.

JOHN   STATEMENT.

"I was born in St. George's in the East. Father died at Rio Janeiro out at sea. He has been dead two years. I have one sister away in America. My mother lives in Albert Street, Back Road. She is a dressmaker. Mother couldn't keep me no longer, so I came in by myself. When I lived with my mother I went to Shadwell Church School."

Education—Can read monosyllables.

BEADLE'S REPORT.
July 30th, 1875.

This boy's father was a ship carpenter. He died 18 months ago of yellow fever at Rio Janeiro, leaving the mother with two children, the above boy, and a girl of 14, who is in Canada. After her husband's death she received what money was due to him, which she soon spent, then took to the streets, and is now living at 27, Albert Street, a common brothel. She walks Ratcliff Highway, and is one of the worst of her kind. She has no regular home, and leaves the boy sometimes for days to get his living as well as he can. On the 20th instant she left him with a woman named Doyle, who keeps three bad houses in Albert Street, who, not hearing anything of his mother, sent him to the Home. Since then I found the mother in a brothel in Betts Street, drunk, with some more prostitutes and sailors. I told her where her boy was, when she said "she did not care where he is; she wished he was dead."

I have made enquiries and find there is no one belonging to him alive except his mother and sister.

Subsequent Report.

1885
Jany 19. Mr Best could not get him to learn farm work. Did not come back to Home. Engaged himself to farmer in the neighbourhood.

Sep. 17. Mr. Duff informed that _____ has met with serious accident in Harvest field having fallen on a hay fork. Is at work again.

17.6.87. John _____ called at the "Home", hoping to see Dr Barnardo. He seems very happy with Mr. Chas. Buck and is earning 12 $ a month.

10.9.87. John _____ called hoping to see Dr Barnardo. He leaves Mr. Buck at the end of November, and is desirous of obtain

No.	Employer	Address	Occupation Employer	Terms	date
1	Best Mr. Wm	Omemee	Farmer	Board & lodging until Spring	12.11.84
2	Reilly Mr	"	"		19.1.85
	Mr Wm Cummings	Enniemore P.O. Co Peterboro			
	Wm Buck	Norwood (Address unknown)	Farmer	85.00 for 7 months	1.2.88

12. *The Doctor kept detailed records of all his young charges.*

13. *The long hours take their toll.*

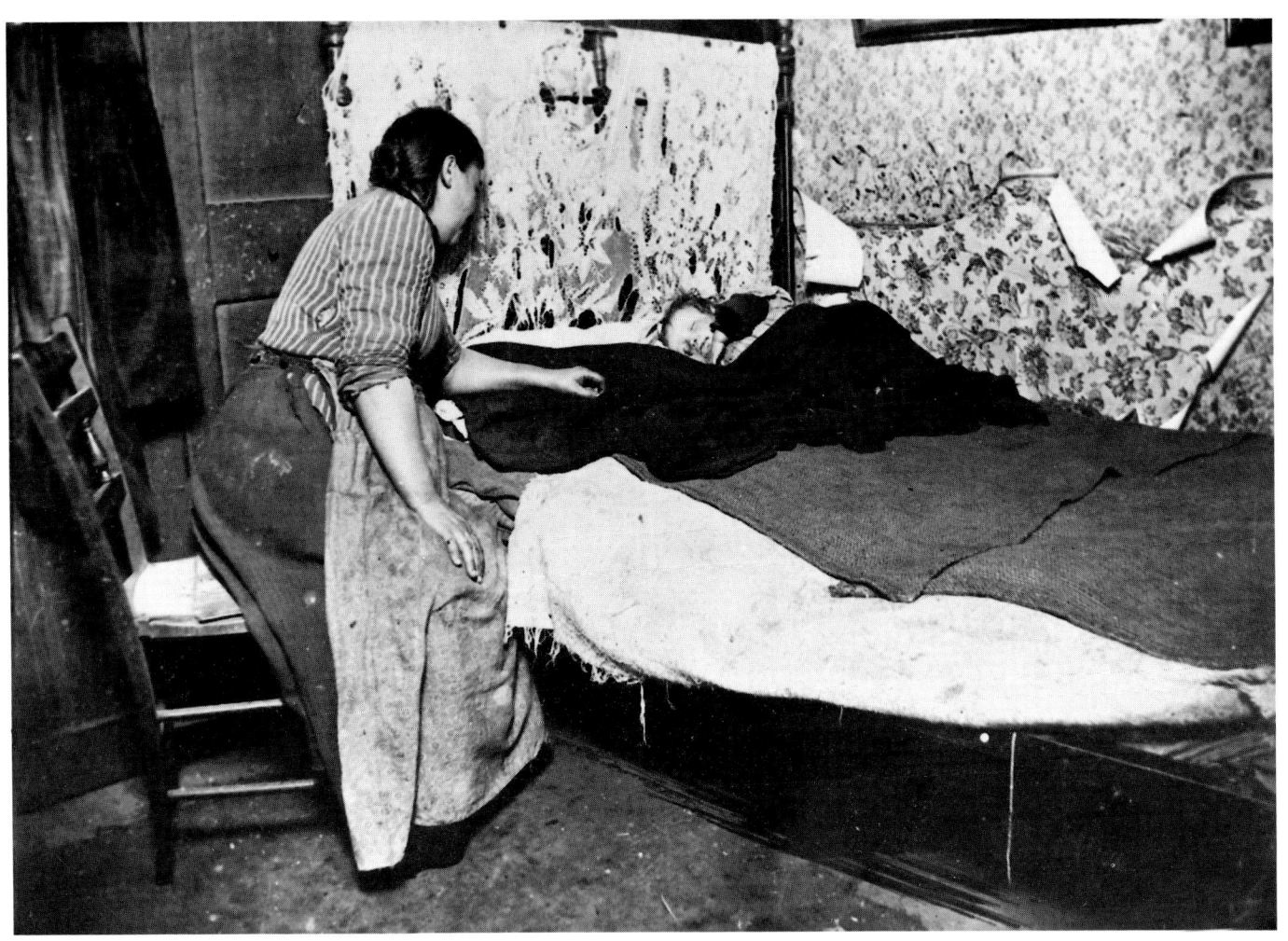

14. Whole families would live in one room.

15. Monotonous making of matchboxes.

16. All the family were expected to work.

THE STREETS OF LONDON . . .

Very often it is foreigners who have the most perceptive eye and some of the more graphic descriptions of London lowlife in the 1860's come from the pen of a French visitor, Hippolyte Taine:

"Beggars, thieves and prostitutes, especially the latter, swarm in Shadwell Street. The grating music from gin cellars can be heard from the street; sometimes the violinist is a negro, and through open windows one sees unmade beds and women dancing. Three times in ten minutes I saw crowds collect round doorways, attracted by fights, especially fights between women. One of them, her face covered with blood, tears in her eyes, drunk, was trying to fly at a man while the mob watched and laughed. And as if the uproar were a signal, the population of neighbouring 'lanes' came pouring into the street, children in rags, paupers, street women, as if a human sewer were suddenly clearing itself.

A few of the women show vestiges of former cleanliness, or wear a new dress; but most of them are in dirty, ill-assorted rags. Imagine what a lady's hat can become after having passed for three or four years from one head to another, been dented against walls, bashed in by blows — for that happens frequently. I noticed numerous black eyes, bandaged noses, cut cheeks. These women gesticulate with extraordinary vehemence; but their most horrible attribute is the voice — thin, shrill, cracked, like that of a sick owl.

It was in this quarter that families were discovered whose only bed was a heap of soot; they had been sleeping on it for some months.

There were swarms of children. At one time, in a narrow alley, I had fourteen or fifteen all around me, dirty, barefoot, one tiny girl carrying an infant, a baby still at breast but whose whitish head was completely bald. Nothing could be more dismal than those livid little bodies, the pale stringy hair, the cheeks of flabby flesh encrusted with old filth . . . Their mothers watched from doorways with dull, uninterested eyes. The interiors were visible, exiguous, sometimes a single room in which a family lives, breathing the foetid air.

The houses are generally of a single storey, low, dilapidated kennels to sleep in and die in. What can it be like in winter when, during weeks of continuous rain and fog, the windows remain closed?

Here and there are rubbish dumps. Women work on them, sorting the rubbish for rags, bones, etc. One of them, old and wrinkled, had a short clay pipe in her mouth; they straightened up and stared at me from the midst of the muck-heap: dull, stupid frightening faces of female yahoos. Perhaps a pipe and a glass of gin is the last thought left in their idiot brains. Is it possible that anything but the instincts and appetites of a savage or a beast of burden can survive in them? A miserable black cat, emaciated, limping, half stupefied, was watching them fearfully out of one eye while furtively sniffing and pawing through a pile of rubbish; no doubt it was right to be nervous — the old woman was watching it with a look as bestial as its own, and mumbling, and it looked to me as if she were thinking that there went two pounds of meat."

17. *The little match girl.*

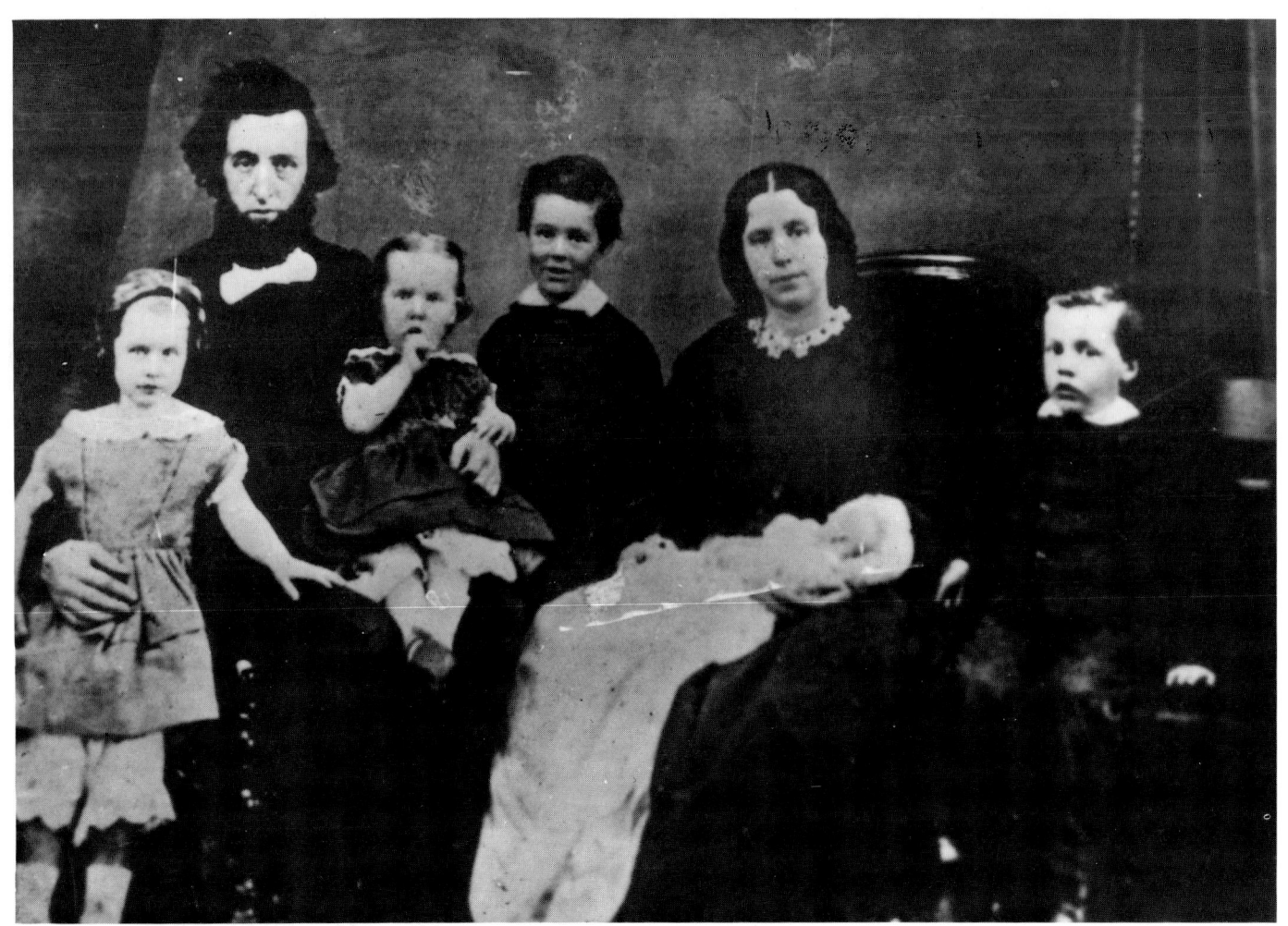

18. William Booth, founder of the Salvation Army, with five of his eight children.

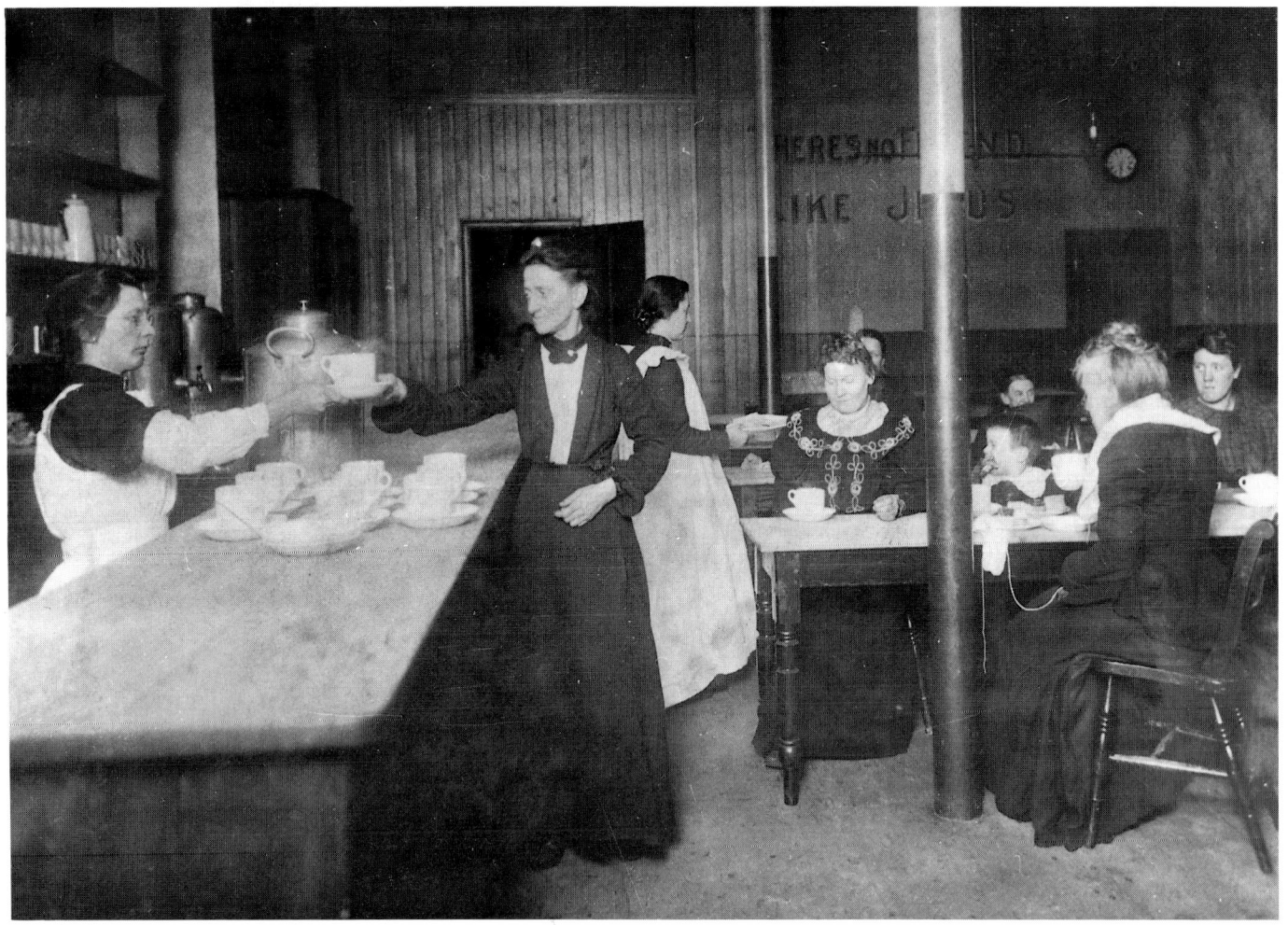

19. At last some support for the poor.

20. *The farthing breakfast. The cup that cheers.*

21. One of the younger charges found on the streets.

Although some fell on stoney ground, many of the Barnardo boys and girls found good jobs both at home and abroad, some eighteen thousand in Canada and Australia. Most of the young girls went into service.

Life on the streets was tough and many deserted children not rescued by Dr. Barnardo had to resort to prostitution to be able to afford a meal. Even those who lived with their parents were often sent out onto the streets to supplement the family income.

THE YOUNG MOTTS

A superintendent of the Metropolitan Police, Joseph Dunlap, was a witness to a committee of the House of Lords who looked into the problem:

Chairman: Do you agree . . . that there is a great deal of juvenile prostitution in the district with which you are more particularly acquainted?

Dunlap: I do.

Chairman: When you use the term "juvenile," what ages do you speak of particularly?

Dunlap: I should say as young as 12 years of age; I should be quite within the bounds of prudence in saying so. Some of them are quite children that are soliciting prostitution in my division.

Chairman: Are these children, of the age of which you speak, living with their parents?

Dunlap: In many instances they are, there is no doubt. I form that opinion from the fact that, when we have been able to charge any of them, they have requested their parents to be informed, or their mothers have sometimes brought them their breakfast to the station; and I have

These conditions so shocked a young man over from Dublin that he abandoned his plans of becoming a medical missionary in China.

What he saw of the East End changed both his life and that of tens of thousands of others. After witnessing the atrocious conditions in which many children were forced to live, sleeping in the gutters, on iron roofs and clad in only the thinnest of rags in all weathers, Dr. Barnardo set about raising money to help the 'street arabs'. Being a gifted orator and tireless worker he opened his first home for destitute lads in Stepney. A Girls' Village Home was later set up in Ilford and the doctor would tirelessly scour the streets, dark alleyways and low lodging houses so he could dramatically improve the lives of young abandoned or orphan children. The philanthropist was a great documenter of all the young people who came into his homes and the excellent photographs are invaluable to any nineteenth century social historian. Although much of this book will deal with what the Doctor would label sin I would like to emphasise that none of the young people featured in the photographs had any direct connection with the capital's more sordid sexual history.

22. Girls were taught to take a pride in their appearance.

23. Dr. Barnardo took many of the photographs himself.

also taken a certain amount of interest in this question, especially with regard to the children, and I have spoken to the mothers when they come, and said to them, "Cannot you get these children out of their wretched life; you know what they are charged with?" They treat the matter, as a rule, indifferently, and will say, "I cannot help it; I have to go out to work; what am I to do?" Then I say, "Then why do you encourage them; why do you not leave the law to deal with them?" They have offered to bring blankets to wrap them up in, which I have invariably refused, and they have offered them every indulgence . . .

Chairman: Generally speaking, where is the prostitution carried on?

Dunlap: In the brothel; there is a low description of brothel in my division, where the children go. I had a warrant to execute a short time ago, to arrest some brothel-keepers, and I went with my chief inspector, and in each of the rooms in that house I found an elderly gentleman in bed with two of these children. I asked their ages, and got into conversation with them. They knew perfectly well that I could not touch them in the house; and they laughed and joked with me, and I could not get any direct answer whatever. I questioned them, in the presence of the brothel-keeper, as to what they had been paid, and so on. They were to receive 6s. each from the gentleman, two of them; and the gentleman had paid 6s. for the room. It was 4s. if there was only one girl, but 6s. if there were two girls for the room. The brothel-keeper was committed for trial.

Chairman: The children were paid by the man?

Dunlap: Yes.

Chairman: And he also paid the brothel-keeper for the room?

Dunlap: Just so.

Chairman: Were the children brought there by the men, or did the children take the men to the particular house?

Dunlap: No doubt the children took the men there.

Lord Penzance: Did the children reside in the house?

Dunlap: No.

Chairman: But they frequented the house?

Dunlap: Yes . . .

Earl Belmore: The other inhabitants of the houses are respectable people, are they not?

Dunlap: Yes, working people; but if they knew that such persons lived there, the difficulty of getting any lodgings is so great that they would have to wink at it a great deal . . .

Lord Alberdare: What is the general cause of the fall of these girls; are they deliberately sent out for this purpose by their parents, or are they procured as customers to particular houses by women in the habit of frequenting the houses?

Dunlap: I do not think it is so. It is only an option; but it appears to me that influence has much to do with it. There are a lot of little servant girls about my division in lodgings, and in other places; they are of every kind; they get small wages; they come out on errands; they see these girls walking about the streets, their equal in social standing; they see them dressed in silks and satins; they do not think of the way they get the money; they say, "You can go and dress in silks and satins while I am slaving"; they talk to the girls, and they are influenced . . .

Lord Leigh: Are they not brought up, the two sexes together, in the same room?'

Dunlap: Yes.

Lord Leigh: And the girls originally came from many of those lodgings?

Dunlap: No doubt.

Lord Leigh: Where several boys and girls mix together?

Dunlap: Yes. There was a case this morning. We had two lads charged at my station with attempting to steal from a carriage in Bond Street, and I saw the "Dialonians," as they are called amongst us, waiting round the station for the police van to come. Amongst them was a little child that had high boots buttoned halfway up her legs; she had very short petticoats, her hair was down her back, and she wore a tight-fitting polonaise. I went outside and endeavoured to get into conversation with her. She thought I had something to do with the police; she said she was waiting to see her man go down. I said, "Has your young man got into trouble; will you come round the street and talk to me?" I thought I might get out some useful information for your Lordships today. She said, "Oh, no." She had her fingers covered with rings; a child of that age.

Chairman: What age did she appear to be?

Dunlap: I should say not above 13. Her fingers were covered with rings. She found I was trying to get information; she laughed, ran down the passage, and waited till "her man" went away in the van, and then hurried up to the police court to see him there.

A SLAP AT THE DEVIL; THE EXTRAORDINARY LIFE OF WILLIAM STEAD

William Stead could only have been a Victorian. He saw the purpose of his life as a fight against the devil yet had adulterous affairs and purchased a young virgin from the streets of the capital. He claimed to have E.S.P. yet bought himself a ticket on the Titanic. He served a prison sentence which he found one of the most enjoyable periods of his life and every year, on November 10, would dress in his prison garb and parade through London. The passionate and excitable religious zealot was not adverse to publicity, indeed it was his job as Stead became one of London's most prolific journalists producing articles that shook the complacent Victorian middle classes to the core.

William was taught to fear hell by his parents in their Northumberland home. He came to believe that every action was directed by God and determined from an early age to devote his life to a fight against Satan. In his diary he noted:

> 'When I see the Devil so strong and his assailants so timorous and half-hearted, I long to be in a place where I can have a full slap at him.'

The chance for confrontation with his arch enemy came when he was offered the post as Editor of the Pall Mall Gazette. In his usual biblical and righteous way he said:

> 'If God needs an Editor of enthusiasm in London, I will serve His turn best.'

The young editor would conveniently forget his religious principles and marriage vows when it suited him and had several affairs, the most notable being with a beautiful and highly intelligent Russian patriot, Olga Novikoff. With his wife he limited intercourse to two times a week for:

> 'If thrice or four times in the week I got deaf with apparent wax formation in the right ear.'

A new variation on the headache, not tonight darling I feel wax in my right ear!

William Stead shook the journalistic world in 1885 with a series of articles about prostitution amongst girls and the trade in the bodies of young virgins. Sometimes journalists report the news, sometimes they make it happen. Stead was a great believer in the second course of action as he set out to prove that young girls could be, and indeed were being, purchased to satisfy a demand for intercourse by anybody who had enough money. No doubt believing his actions were being directed by God, Stead set out to 'buy' a young virgin.

Calling himself Charles and applying rouge to his face, the man who had never been to the theatre began to frequent some of the capital's more fashionable places, smoking cigars and drinking champagne, even though he found both repugnant. In many ways Stead was as a journalist far ahead of his time. Unfortunately the following events led to the disgrace and humiliation of everybody concerned.

To prove his theory about the wide scale sale of young girls, Stead determined to purchase one for himself, though he of course would not carry out the sexual act. He needed contacts in the 'underworld' from whence most of the victims were produced. The 'way in' was via Rebecca Jarrett. When he first met her, Rebecca was in her forties and walked with a very bad limp caused by a hip becoming diseased after a fall. In her youth she had been in service and followed a familiar path of being seduced by one of the house-guests and gradually drifting into a life of prostitution. She later set up her own brothel to supply 'virgins' and took to the bottle. Rebecca discovered God and became what we would probably call today a born again Christian as she took to preaching in pubs. When informed of Stead's plans to show it was possible to buy a virgin she agreed to help him and went to visit the brothels she knew to see if there were any available.

Eliza Armstrong had long black hair partly hidden by a straw hat, its yellow feather contrasting with the new purple dress. She met Stead and they had a cup of tea before proceeding to an accommodation house over a ham and beef shop in Poland Street. Let's leave the editor himself to continue the story in the Pall Mall Gazette of July 6, 1885. The readers did not know that Stead himself was the 'purchaser' and several of the details were to be proved untrue:

24. Crowded conditions in the East End.

A CHILD OF THIRTEEN BOUGHT FOR £5

"Let me conclude the chapter of horrors by one incident, and only one of those which are constantly occurring in those dread regions of subterranean vice in which sexual crime flourishes almost unchecked. I can personally vouch for the absolute accuracy of every fact in the narrative.

"At the beginning of this Derby week, a woman, an old hand in the work of procuration, entered a brothel in _____ St., M_____, kept by an old acquaintance, and opened negotiations for the purchase of a maid. One of the women who lodged in the house had a sister as yet untouched. Her mother was far away, her father was dead. The child was living in the house, and in all probability would be seduced and follow the profession of her elder sister. The child was between thirteen and fourteen, and after some bargaining it was agreed that she should be handed over to the procuress for the sum of £5 . . .

"The next day, Derby Day as it happened, was fixed for the delivery of this human chattel. But as luck would have it, another sister of the child who was to be made over to the procuress heard of the proposed sale. She was living respectably in a situation, and on hearing of the fate reserved for the little one she lost no time in persuading her dissolute sister to break off the bargain. When the woman came for her prey the bird had flown. Then came the chance of Lily's mother. The brothel-keeper sent for her, and offered her a sovereign for her daughter. The woman was poor, dissolute, and indifferent to everything but drink. The father, who was also a drunken man, was told his daughter was going to a situation. He received the news with indifference, without even inquiring where she was going to. The brothel-keeper having thus secured possession of the child, then sold her to the procuress in place of the child whose sister had rescued her from her destined doom for £5 — £3 paid down and the remaining £2 after her virginity had been professionally certified. The little girl, all unsuspecting the purpose for which she was destined, was told that she must go with this strange woman to a situation . . .

"The first thing to be done after the child was fairly severed from home was to secure the certificate of virginity without which the rest of the purchase-money would not be forthcoming. In order to avoid trouble she was taken in a cab to the house of a midwife, whose skill in pronouncing upon the physical evidences is generally recognised in the profession. The examination was very brief and completely satisfactory. But the youth, the complete innocence of the girl, extorted pity even from the hardened heart of the old abortionist. 'The poor little thing,' she exclaimed. 'She is so small, her pain will be extreme. I hope you will not be too cruel with her' — as if to lust when fully roused the very acme of agony on the part of the victim has not a fierce delight. To quiet the old lady the agent of the purchaser asked if she could supply anything to dull the pain. She produced a small phial of chloroform. 'This,' she said, 'is the best. My clients find this much the most effective.' The keeper took the bottle, but unaccustomed to anything but drugging by the administration of sleeping potions, she would infallibly have poisoned the child had she not discovered by experiment that the liquid burned the mouth when an attempt was made to swallow it. £1 1s. was paid for the certificate of virginity — which was verbal and not written — while £1 10s. more was charged for the chloroform, the net value of which was probably less than a shilling. An arrangement was made that if the child was badly injured Madame would patch it up to the best of her ability, and then the party left the house.

"From the midwife's the innocent girl was taken to a house of ill fame, No. _____, P_____-street, Regent-street, where, notwithstanding her extreme youth, she was admitted without question. She was taken upstairs, undressed, and put to bed, the woman who bought her putting her to sleep. She was rather restless, but under the influence of chloroform she soon went over. Then the woman withdrew. All was quiet and still. A few moments later the door opened, and the purchaser entered the bedroom. He closed and locked the door. There was a brief silence. And then there rose a wild and piteous cry — not a loud shriek, but a helpless, startled scream like the bleat of a frightened lamb. And the child's voice was heard crying, in accents of terror. 'There's a man in the room! Take me home; oh, take me home!' . . .

And then all once more was still.

"That was but one case among many, and by no means the worst. It only differs from the rest because I have been able to verify the facts. Many a similar cry will be raised this very night in the brothels of London, unheeded by man, but not unheard by the pitying ear of Heaven —

"For the child's sob in the darkness curseth deeper
Than the strong man in his wrath."

The description of both parents was far from the truth and many details were deliberately left out. Stead painted as black a picture as he could of everybody involved in the sorry episode. When Eliza's parents read the account they knew immediately that it concerned their daughter and were not surprisingly very indignant with Mrs. Armstrong complaining to Scotland Yard. As today, there was great rivalry amongst the newspapers especially as the Gazette's circulation had rocketed, and Mrs. Armstrong did not have to search far for help in her complaints against Stead, the case being taken up by a reporter from Lloyd's Newspaper.

In the meantime after her ordeal of being chloroformed and finding a man in her room Eliza was sent to a doctor to confirm that Stead had not had his wicked way with her. Eliza was sent to Paris, returning a short time later and discovered in Stead's garden. He had not sought permission from her parents to send her abroad and the police were becoming more and more interested in the case. In his own headstrong manner the editor had not considered the effects of the ordeal on the young girl; being examined twice to prove her virginity, taken to a strange house, chloroformed and eventually sent abroad.

For their part in the sordid events, Madame Mourez, who confirmed the girl's virginity, and Rebecca Jarrett who procured the victim, were each sentenced to six months imprisonment. Stead was ordered to serve three months. He enjoyed special privileges inside with his own armchair, comfortable bed, desk and 'cosy little tea table.' He wrote 'Never had I a happier lot than the months I spent in happy Holloway.'

Every November 10th he would take the train to Waterloo and walk across the bridge in his prison clothes. Stead returned to the Gazette with the proviso that there were to be no more 'virgins' but left shortly after and if you are ever asked to name the passenger list of the Titanic, you could now name at least one person.

25. William Stead fought a one-man battle against the Devil.

'WELL DONE, THOU GOOD AND FAITHFUL SERVANT'

There were only two possibilities of earning a living for some girls; domestic service or prostitution.

The standards expected of servants in the mid-nineteenth century meant that employees were almost slaves without chains, their sole reason for being was to serve their master or mistress.

The following guidelines were printed in 'The New Female Instructor' under the title 'Advice to servants.'

'She always looks clean and tidy; even when dressed in a close bedgown, and a plain linen or cotton cap, she is doing dirty work. She is never seen about the house with holes in her stockings, or slipshod shoes, or a tattered gown, or blowzy hair, or dirty hands . . . When she buys new clothes, she always considers whether they are of a reasonable price, and likely to last long; and are proper for a person in her situation.

The good servant never desires to go to races, or feasts, or fairs, or any merrymakings; never spends any time or money, on silly books or songs; or in running after fortune-tellers; or in buying lottery-tickets. She never plays at cards: she does not want to get other people's money from them, and she does not want to lose her own. A walk in her master's garden or in the fields, either by herself, or with sober company; a visit to her friends; or a good book to read; are the amusements which she likes best.

She never invites or encourages any company to come and see her at her master's house, not even her own relations without first asking leave . . . She is no tattler, nor busybody, nor talebearer, gossiping about from house to house, speaking things which she ought not. She does not want to find out other people's secrets, or to tell those of the family in which she lives. She would grieve very much if she thought that her master and mistress, or any of their family, looked upon her as a spy, or as an enemy, glad to take every little opportunity to speak ill of them, or to do them any unkindness.

Every morning and every evening, she prays to the great God, to bless her, and her master and mistress, and all their family; and daily she reads some portion of the Holy Scriptures. She delights to follow her master and mistress, and their children to the house of God.'

There was often no love lost between servants and their employers and stories of loyal and hardworking butlers and housekeepers were more likely to be the stuff of fiction. An eighteenth century advertisement of a sarcastic nature shows how some employers viewed their staff:

'A maid-servant to be hired, either weekly, monthly or quarterly, for reasonable wages. One that is an incomparable slut, and goes all the day slip-shod with her stockings out at heels; an excellent house-wife, that wastes more of everything than she spends; an egregious scold, that will always have the last word; an everlasting gossip, that tells abroad whatsoever is done in the house; a lazy trollop, that cares not how late she sits up, nor how long she lies in the morning; and in short, one that is light-fingered, knowing nothing and yet pretending to know everything.'

There was a great deal of dissatisfaction with servants not matching their employers' expectations. The poem ''A Good Servant' outlines the kind of behaviour not tolerated by the rich, but one's sympathy and understanding must go to the near-slaves who worked long hours for a pittance.

Wouldst thou a household servant be,
Three points of character I see
Needful for thriving — these the three:

Be sober, honest, and discreet,
Or no good mistress wilt thou meet;
And be in person clean and neat.

Three things avoid with special care;
Tales from your master's house to bear,
For once out they fly everywhere;

Avoid strong drink, for none can know
How fast the love of it may grow,
And then disgrace will not be slow;

Scraps give not to your friends away
Unless your mistress says you may —
Their greed will grow till it betray.

Three things in household service too
'Twere well that thou shouldst ably do,
Though all may be well done by few:

Scrub well, cook well and well attend
Then will thy mistress be thy friend,
And make thee happy in the end.

Scrub well the floors and make them white,
Polish the tables, shining bright,
Rub all the glasses clear as light.

With noiseless step and watchful eye,
Whate'er the guests may want supply,
Making no bustle needlessly.

Still three rules more must thou observe
If thou perfectly wouldst serve,
And praise and honour well deserve:

If you do wrong the error own,
Nothing hide that should be known,
Or conceal what should be shown.

Never let idle vanity
Tempt you your ladies' clothes to try,
Or in their drawers and cupboards pry.

Let all things in their places be,
That none need seek what all should see;
And aim at punctuality.

Such, then, as all these things can do
We reckon servants good and true;
Pity there should be so few!

Not surprisingly many thousands were tempted to the richer pickings available on the streets.

After looking at the atrocious conditions in which young girls were forced to live and their poor prospects of ever earning a decent living wage, it is easy to understand the financial attractions of prostitution. When faced with the choice of living with drunken parents in an overcrowded slum with only scraps to eat and rags to wear, and the better conditions found in some brothels, it was no surprise that many girls chose the latter path.

Girls going out to Service.

In the earnest hope of encouraging girls in the Village Home to aim at a higher standard of conduct, and at the same time to prevent those who do badly from sharing, as they have hitherto done, in those benefits which only the well-conducted deserve, the Director has laid down the following conditions upon which alone in future Village Home girls will be placed out in service.

All girls who have reached their thirteenth birthday are placed in one or other of four divisions, according to character and conduct. The conditions of their going out to service are determined by the class in which they stand. A special review of these classes is made every six months, and the names of girls are transferred from any one division to any other as they have shown improvement or the reverse.

These four classes are as under:—

FIRST DIVISION All girls who on attaining their sixteenth year have a record of conduct and character which has been uniformly good for two years, will be eligible for going out to service at once, or as soon as suitable situations can be obtained for them. They will be furnished with an oufit of the first class, value £5, which will become their own, free of any charge, if they keep their first situation twelve months. Furthermore in the event of their keeping their first situation twelve months with a good character, they will be entitled to receive a special prize.

SECOND DIVISION Girls who have frequently given way to ill temper, disobedience, insolence, laziness or other grave faults within two years of their going out to service, cannot be placed in the first division; but if a resolute endeavour is observed in them to overcome their faults, and if, during the last twelve months of their stay in the Village, there is decided improvement, they will be placed in the second division, and receive a second class outfit, value £3 10s., which will become their own property on the same conditions as in the first division. Second division girls will also receive a prize if they keep their first situation with a good character, for twelve months.

THIRD DIVISION Girls who up to the time of their leaving for service continue to exhibit bad conduct, ill-temper, self-will, disobedience or insolence can only be placed out in the third division, the Mistress being informed of their faults. They will receive a third class outfit, value £3, the whole of which must be paid for out of their own wages. A girl in the third division will not be eligible for a prize till she has been two years in service, and has earned a good character.

FOURTH DIVISION Girls who are found to be dishonest, habitually untruthful, violent and uncontrolled in temper, vicious, unclean in their personal habits, will not be sent out to service under ordinary circumstances, nor will they have an outfit, but will be dismissed from the Village in disgrace or sent to a School of discipline.

GIRLS' VILLAGE HOME, ILFORD.   *T. J. BARNARDO.*

26. Relegation from the fourth division usually led to a life on the streets.

27. *The Share-out. Prostitutes often doubled-up as pickpockets.*

A WALK ON THE WILD SIDE: THE PATH TO PROSTITUTION

There was no shortage of madams on the lookout for new recruits. In the eighteenth century Mother Whyburn would do the rounds of the taverns 'to see what Youth and Beauty the Countrey had sent to London.' A bible in her hand she would then proceed to the prisons and bribe the jailer to release 'the finest kitlings.' The day was finished off with a trip to the 'children market' outside St.-Martin-in-the-Fields. Those who met her approval after an examination such as 'A Butcher might chuse a Mare at Smithfield' were cleaned up, painted, patched and hired out as parsons' daughters to customers at her brothels.

To attract customers the girls needed to be cleaner and wear better clothes than they had in their slum life so the madams would feed and clothe their workers. Mother Willit of Gerrard Street spoke of one of the madams:

> 'So help her kidnies, she al'us turned her girls out with a clean arse and a good tog;'

Elizabeth Needham had a ready market for the girls she encouraged into prostitution as her main customer was Colonel Francis Charteris, 'the Rapemaster-General of the Kingdom.' The law caught up with the procuress and such was the hatred of the mob that she died a few days after her stand in the pillory.

An anonymous author was so shocked by the state of the streets of London that in 1749 he published a book to illustrate the problems and hopefully remedy them. He certainly succeeded in the first aim but failed miserably in the second. The title of his book probably appealed more to those interested in what the author saw as a low and ungodly life. "Satan's Harvest Home; or the Present State of Whorecraft, Adultery, Fornication, Pimping, Sodomy, etc." He describes Drury Lane:

> *"Turn your eyes up to the Chambers of Wantonness, and you behold the most shameful scenes of Lewdness in the windows even at Noon-day, some in the very act of Vititation (intercourse) visible to all the opposite Neighbours. Others dabbing their shifts, aprons and headcloths, and exposing themselves just naked to the Passers by . . . You hear at the Corner of every Court, Lane and Avenue, the Quarrels and Outcries of Harlots recriminating one another, Soldiers and Bullies intermixing, the most execrable Oaths are heard . . ."*

In Norton Street, Marylebone, prostitutes often appeared at the window naked, lounged on the window sills and ran into the street wearing only one undergarment to drag men in.

Europeans were fascinated by the Capital's night life and went into details about the modus operandi of prostitutes. Archenoltz notes:

> *"So soon as it becomes dark, these girls, well turned-out, in all seasons flood the principal streets and squares of the town. Many go on the man-hunt in borrowed clothes which they hire by the day from the matrons, who for safety's sake pay another woman to follow the huntress continuously on foot in order to see that she does not run away with the clothes. If the girl makes no capture and comes home without money, she will be ill-treated and*

must go hungry. They therefore accost passers-by and take them either home or to taverns. They can be seen standing in groups. The best class of prostitutes, who live independently, are content to go on their way until they are spoken to. Many married women even, who live in distant parts of the town, come to the Westminster district where they are unknown and carry on the profession either from vice or need. I have been astounded to see children of eight and nine years offer their company, at least as far as it would serve. The corruption of men's hearts is so great, that even such children can find lovers to flirt with them. More than that: at midnight the girls leave the streets and old beggar women of 60 and more come out from their hiding places in order to serve drunken men returning heated from their revels, who must satisfy their animal needs blindly, as it were 'at the gallop'."

A very similar description is furnished by Schütz:

"So soon as the streets are lamp-lighted, which lighting is not regulated by the changes of the moon, but by the fall of darkness, they begin to swarm with street girls who, well got-up and well dressed, display their attractions. Certain it is that no place in the world can be compared with London for wantonness, and even the strictest observer of chastity has many temptations to fight against; the number of evening and night prowlers is so unbelievable. Many of them stroll the streets alone, and it must be said to their credit that they are fairly discreet. Either they silently offer one their arm or they make use of all sorts of formulas such as, for instance:

"I should so much like to marry you."
"Your love would make me happy."

Little had changed one hundred years later. Firstly Taine's notes on England:

"I recall the lanes which open off Oxford Street, stifling alleys thick with human effluvia, troops of pale children crouching on filthy staircases; the street benches at London Bridge where all night whole families huddle close, heads hanging, shaking with cold; above all I recall Haymarket and the Strand at evening, where you cannot walk a hundred yards without knocking into twenty street-walkers; some of them ask you for a glass of gin; others say, "It's for my rent mister." The impression is not one of debauchery but of abject, miserable poverty... It seemed as if I were watching a march past of dead women."

Walter in 'My Secret Life' probably the most pornographic book published in the nineteenth century, tells us of his personal experiences. This extract is from the censored version published by Grafton books. We shall hear more of the anonymous author and his uncensored works a little later:

"Going one Saturday night up Granby Street, Waterloo Road, then full of women who used to sit at the windows half naked; two or three together at times in the same room on the ground-floor, with the bed visible from the street, and which street I often walked in for the pleasure of looking at the women. A woman standing at the door seized my hand asking me in and at the same time pulling me quite violently into the little passage. I had barely seen her, and upon her saying, 'Come and have me,' replied that I scarcely had any money. 'Never mind' said she, 'we will have it for all that.' She shut the door, closed rapidly the other wooden shutters, which all the ground-floor windows had in that

28. *The Wages of Sin.*

29. There's nothing like the real thing.

street, and began to kiss and feel me. I then saw she was half drunk. Quickly she pulled me towards the bed, threw herself on it.

'I can't do it,' said I in fright, for her manner was so lewed, and became so ferocious, that it quite upset me. 'What! a fine young man like you can't do it,' said she. 'No' (and as an apology) 'I often can't do it.' 'I will give you a pleasure' said she. 'I can if anyone can,' and, although it disgusted me, she dropped to her knees saying;

'a man can always do it one way or another.'

That over, she rose and said, 'You will come to me again, won't you? I will always do that for you and anything else you like.' I gave her a shilling and promised, but never felt so sick and disgusted with a woman before. Everything about the woman was repulsive. I avoided the street for some months, which was a great loss to me, for I often used to go through it to gloat on the charms of the women as they lolled out of the windows."

In the docklands the women known as 'Sailor's tarts' had their own individual style of dress. Few wore hats though nets were sometimes employed. Dresses were low-cut and decorated with sham flowers and multi-coloured ribbons. The pink or white stockings encased in Morocco boots with polished brass heels were particularly attractive to the sailor who may have spent months without seeing a member of the opposite sex.

They were looking forward to their arrival in port and trip to the Ratcliffe Highway where they would soon be surrounded by loud-voiced and buxom women parading in groups. Nights of dancing, drinking and fornication would inevitably leave them broke and having to return to their ships. The dancing would take place in a room above a public house. The music from fiddles, fifes and cornets inspired the 'couples' to dance the polka or waltz in a frenzied drunken manner. Sometimes the sailor would go back to the tart's house and find himself penniless in the morning, but more often than not the nearest dark alley and a quick knee-trembler satisfied both the sailor's sexual needs and woman's financial ones.

Black Sarah 'the far-famed mollisher' was one of the most popular and talked-about prostitutes in the Ratcliffe Highway at the start of Victoria's reign. There were no stipulations as to the colour, race or creed of her customers and 'The Town' described her as:

> "A Dutch-built piratical schooner carrying on a free trade under the black flag . . . many and many a stout and lusty lugger has borne down upon, and hoisted the British standard over, our sable privateer, Black Sall."

There was even a short verse written about her:

> The lady with diamonds and laces,
>   By day may heighten her charms,
> But Sall without any graces,
>   At night lies as warm in your arms.
>
> The night when her sable o'ershades us,
>   Will veil all the pomp of the day,
> Then Sall is as good as my lady,
>   And cats are all equally grey.

30. Black Sall.

31. Lobby loungers. The theatres were the most popular haunts for prostitutes.

KITTY FISHER AND BREAKFAST OF A £50 NOTE

Not all life was sleazy and there were rich pickings to be made by some of the capital's more charismatic young ladies.

Kitty was a beautiful girl. Her ripe, provoking lips and saucy tilted nose gave her face an expression of roguery. The blue-grey eyes and youthful appearance were attracting men from all over the capital to the milliner's shop. These beaux would buy a ribbon or pair of gloves but really they came to flirt with the poor silver-chaser's daughter.

Faced with a choice between the drudgery of shop work and a life of luxury she, understandably, chose the latter and after appearing in all public places, engaged in a series of affairs which very rapidly pushed her up the social ladder. She was a familiar face in the boxes of the theatre, at masked balls and wandering through the parks and pleasure gardens.

Ms. Fisher made the most of her trim figure by purchasing the most expensive and fashionable clothes supplemented by a straw hat with upturned brim and waving ribbons. Just a few years after leaving the milliner's, Kitty Fisher had become a celebrity; the most pretty, extravagant, wicked little wanton that ever flourished. She was greatly admired and desired by all such as preferred the joys of sexual contact to all the other pleasures of life.

Kitty enjoyed the notoriety and after several portraits of her were painted she could charge as much as one hundred guineas per night as the price of her favours. Despite this sum being a fortune for the mid-eighteenth century there were plenty of admirers who did not seem to be discouraged by this large amount.

Kitty spent her wealth on gowns, jewellery and her stately coach drawn by four grey horses. It was only a matter of time before members of the Royal family started to take an interest in the capital's most notorious inhabitant. The Duke of York, who was in the habit of chasing every pretty young woman, was invited to take tea at her house in New Norfolk Street. When he left the next morning, the brother of the Heir Apparent only left a present of £50. Kitty gave orders that he was not be be re-admitted and rumour has it that she sent the banknote to a pastrycook who put it into a tartlet which she later ate for breakfast.

There were often farcical situations arising because of the number of friends that Kitty used to entertain. On one day the diminutive Lord Montfort arrived to find Kitty in full dress, patched and powdered, ready for the opera. As the Lord was such a rich patron she agreed to give him a short interview but almost immediately heard the arrival of Lord Sandwich, her escort for the evening. There was no cupboard or curtain in the room, and Kitty, anxious that the two should not meet, resorted to the only hiding place available. Raising one of the corners of her hoop-petticoat, she commanded the Lord to slip underneath. With the nobleman cosily concealed under one of the huge panniers, the Earl of Sandwich entered the apartment.

Apparently unaffected by the presence under her dress Kitty engaged in small talk before being asked to be excused that she might fetch her cloak. Whispering "keep close" she swept from the room and deposited the smiling Lord Montfort in the adjoining boudoir.

Not everybody was enamoured of Kitty's charms and Casanova who introduced himself with the words 'I love you,' the only English words he knew, wrote that she "prattled like a magpie, the hissing almost made him giddy."

The scandal surrounding Kitty's life led to civil disturbance in the capital when her proud coachman, Matthew Dodd, was arrested on the charge of assaulting a Miss Anne Dutnall, the daughter of a Surrey farmer. The complainant was described as: "a very sensible, modest, well-behaved girl of nineteen, whose case was very affecting." Found guilty, Kitty's coachman was

32. Kitty Fisher. A taste for money.

ordered to be hanged. Popular feeling was against this very harsh sentence, as it was thought the case for the prosecution had been exaggerated.

On Friday, the 19th August, Matthew Dodd was led from the New Gaol to pay the penalty of his crime. An incensed mob was waiting and gathering around the cart, they made a frantic attempt to rescue the prisoner. It was only with great difficulty that the jailors managed to get him back to his cell. At six o'clock that evening a company of infantry arrived from the Tower. With an escort of 150 soldiers, bayonets fixed, the cortege set out for Kennington Common. The prisoner's poor wife, who had been waiting all day for a last glimpse of her husband, let out several high pierced shrieks when he came into view, inciting the crowd to a second attempt at rescue. The mob, many of whom had been bribed by Kitty, made a valiant attempt but by seven-thirty Matthew was dancing the Paddington frisk.

Kitty Fisher had been London's number one female attraction for six years, had several portraits painted, books of a dubious nature written about her, and all sorts of nonsense in the press. Tiring of the life Kitty married John Norris and moved to Kent. This period of her life was probably the happiest she had ever known, spending all day in the saddle of her coal-black mare, Kitty, she became a well-respected figure in the local community.

In spite of exercise and fresh air, Kitty began to lose strength day by day. The reformed young woman knew she was going to die and towards the end of her days found solace in religion, hoping to obtain pardon for what were in those days considered to be sins. With her husband's arms around her, after just the shortest of marriages and in her twenty-ninth year, she passed quietly to her rest.

THE BIRD OF PARADISE

Gertrude Tilson stood 4' 1" in her stockinged feet and had a passion for bright clothes, her caps and gowns being of the most vivid hues. When she was launched upon London life at the age of sixteen, there were few of either sex who did not stop to admire her. She was seen as "the dearest little doll or plaything." Her figure being shapely and in full perfect proportion, the complexion brilliant and features piquant, having a smile for everyone and attending all social functions, she would be found at the centre of a group of admiring beaux; all were convinced that she would marry a rich suitor.

Gilbreath Mahon was a gambler. Having been captivated by Gertrude's beauty, he had not been able to stop himself from gawking at her throughout the church service. The Irishman decided to show his hand, and following several clandestine meetings where Gilbreath would sing and enchant the young girl, he proposed marriage. The Bird of Paradise as the young lady was to become known due to her fondness of bright clothing, accepted without enquiring into her beau's financial affairs. It was doubtful whether the young man even had a shilling in his pocket as, following a brief career as a musician, he had fallen in with bullies and dice-players and led a hand-to-mouth existence.

Knowing her mother totally opposed to the union, the couple, head-over-heels in love, decided to flee to France. In October 1769, Gertrude left a note for her mother and like countless thousands of girls in the past and as thousands will do in the future, left her monotonous home for a life of adventure on the road. She was soon to learn what a wild world was waiting. Her mother was a hard-headed woman who immediately dispatched two Bow Street Runners to intercept the couple at Dover, the Bird of Paradise being a minor.

33. The Bird of Paradise.

The unsuspecting lovers were apprehended in their hotel but Gilly, a gambler, had one or two tricks up his sleeve. Being exhausted, the young Irishman admitted the game was up and pleaded that his beloved should be allowed to retire to her room. He would remain in their company and maybe have one or two drinks for the road. Like many Irish, Gilly was a born story-teller and charmer, and was soon having the runners in fits of laughter with his banter. He would refrain from consuming most of his drink, and when the police had finally drunk themselves under the table, he went to join Gertrude who had flown to one of the longer boats, after escaping down a ladder.

The Bow Street Runners gave chase to France but after a series of legal disputes were told to leave the country, and miles from nowhere, the couple were married on the first of November.

It was only a short time later that practicalities like money clouded their ideal life. The couple returned to London and the Bird of Paradise flew back to her nest. A second marriage was held in London and a baby son born a few months later. Gertrude's mother would never accept her son-in-law as part of the family and he found himself a social outcast in the capital. Disillusioned, he returned to the dice and cards and set out to seek a fresh fortune in the shape of the heiress Miss Russell. Once again the Irishman set out for the continent with an attractive lady but the woman he had left behind had tired of him; with the death of her mother the Bird of Paradise determined on a new life — that of a society lady, or high-class prostitute.

Gertrude adored the masked balls and was an immediate hit dressed in gorgeous finery, wearing a perpetual smile. After several flattering reports in society newspapers, the Bird of Paradise was to become the latest toast of 'evening' world. Such was her passion for night-life and enjoying herself that the recently-deserted wife would attend the more tawdry masquerades and more often than not found herself voted the belle of the ball. She would spend these evenings singing and entertaining 'loose women and their paramours.'

Given her nickname by one of the newspapers she would mix with other 'birds'. The newspapers seemed to be into white with a 'White Swan' and a 'White Crow' who were often spotted with the 'Goldfinch' or 'Waterwagtail.' The Bird of Paradise however was the star attraction at the balls and in the parks. Both father and son would turn their heads to admire her, wearing 'an elegant and simple dress, the modern cestus around her waist, and her hair of the finest jet combed in ringlets without the least shade of white or red powder.'

The press could not print enough about the diminuitive sweetheart and would report her every move. Like journalists today they would praise a character one week only to decry them the next:

> 'The Bird of Paradise' is seen hopping about in rather a disconsolate manner. We hear she has had too much saffron administered in the waters of her cage lately.'

> 'The little 'Bird of Paradise' is said by some to have been moulting, by others to be laid up with the pip ...'

> 'The 'Bird of Paradise' appeared at Vauxhall in glittering plumage, her waist not a span round, her stature four feet one inch, with black hair truly Mahomedan, delicately arched eye-brows smooth as mouse skin, and soft pouting lips.''

Gertrude was very careful with her money, as one reporter commented:

> 'The Hen of Paradise though no larger than a canary can swallow gold and silver with the facility of an ostrich.'

Over the next few years Gertrude Mahon prospered. Her appearance on the stage caused every seat to be sold. She had a string of rich male friends and was often spotted in a French yellow coach and silver-plated harness. Gertrude invested heavily in clothes in pursuit of the one prey that so far eluded her, the Prince of Wales. Whenever George attended the opera, Gertrude adorned herself in her most daring costumes and took great care to appear in her own private box and in the park after the show.

The rumour that the Prince had tired of 'Dally the Tall' proved to be true and he ventured from one extreme to another, frequently being found entertained at the house of the 'Bird of Paradise'. Gertrude Mahon had reached the height of the social scene, though rumours spread that the Prince had not rewarded her with a present, as was the custom, George soon found new friends and Gertrude ceased to interest reporters as much as she once had. Her husband was now back in Britain in a debtors prison. The 'Bird of Paradise' continued to frequent the capital's night spots, both high and low, but by thirty-four her beauty was fading. The young lady who had appeared as a painted doll in the Temple of Venus and had been cited in divorce cases, just seemed to fade away, to such an extent that there is not even a record of the death of the woman, once London's number one attraction.

Both Kitty and Gertrude spent a great deal of their income on their appearance and new fashions have never ceased to shock the capital.

FEMALE FASHION; PATCHES, PETTICOATS AND PADDING

34. The covering or uncovering of breasts. A controversial topic in the fashion world.

35. Wool, laces, ribbons, ostrich feathers and pastes were added to achieve the required style.

"I like silk stockings well, because they are pleasant, fine and delicate, and henceforth I shall wear no more cloth stockings."

Despite her black teeth and need for red wigs, Elizabeth I took great pride in her appearance. The fair sex were often attacked in print by men who did not consider the final result worthy of the time and energy expended.

In 1593 Nash insulted fashionable ladies:

> 'Theur heads, with their top and top-gallant lawn baby-caps, and snow — resembled silver curlings, they make a plain puppet stage of. Their breasts they embusk up on high, and their round roseate buds immodestly lay forth to show at their hands there is fruit to be hoped in their curious anti-woven garments, they imitate and mock the worms and adders that must eat them. They shew the swellings of their mind, in the swellings and plumpings out of their apparel. Gorgeous ladies of court, never wer I admitted so near any of you, as to see how you torture old time with sponging, pinning, and pouncing; but they say his sickle you have burst in twain, to make your periwigs more elevated arches of.'

In the 1600s patches were very popular, with Whig ladies wearing them on the right side of the face and Tories on the left. Those undecided or plainly not interested in politics wore them on both cheeks.

Pepys observed Lady Castlemaine at the theatre call an attendant 'for a little patch off her face, and put it into her own mouth and wetted it, and so clapped it upon her own by the side of her mouth. I suppose she felt a pimple rising there.'

Doctor Graham's splendidly furnished Temple of Health has been discussed in "Wicked London". He also gave lectures on health and beauty, very popular with female audiences. Those who attended were often ashamed of letting it be known and would therefore sport masks.

A chair would be placed in the middle of the lecture-room, surrounded by a small pit, half full of earth. Half-naked, the doctor would make his entrance and seat himself on the chair. Two employees would then fill the pit with more earth. As the level of the soil rose higher, so too would the doctor's shirt. Once the earth reached his chest Graham would discard his chemise completely, and have the earth arranged so that only his head remained on view. By now completely naked, he would lecture on the virtues of mother earth and its benefits for the pores of the skin and the stimulation of the blood.

The fashion for built-up coiffures first became popular in the 1700s. Wool, laces, ribbons, ostrich feathers, curls, combs, pins, pastes and false hair were added to the natural hair so that a woman might be one third taller when she left the hairdresser.

Addison comments:

> 'About ten years ago approximately, it shot up to a very great height, insomuch that the female part of species was much taller than the men. The women were of such enormous stature that we appeared as grasshoppers before them. At present the species is in a manner dwarfed and shrunk. I remember several ladies, who were once very nearly seven feet high, that at present want some inches of five.'

The covering, or uncovering of the breasts has proved a controversial topic in the world of fashion for centuries. Although going topless is almost seen as the norm on most Mediterranean beaches today books against the fashion of exposing bare breasts were published in the seventeenth century. The Queen of England was one of the exponents of the fashion in 1672 when a book with the following title was published; 'New instructions to Youth as to their Behaviour, together with a discussion of some Novelties in the Mode; against powdering the Hair, Naked Breasts and Patches, and other unseemly customs.'

One of the pictures features a woman with two enormous breasts protruding from a low corset. The face is of course disfigured and covered with patches. Two more books appeared: 'A just and reasonable Reprehension of naked Breasts and shoulders' and 'England's vanity; or the voice of God against the monstrous sin of Pride in Dress and Apparel.'

With the eighteenth century came the fashion for false breasts. These were made of wax but the wearer had to be particularly careful not to make a boob as was the case in the following story from 'the school of fashion':

'A young lady who was to be married in a few days' time to a worthy man, was with her betrothed at the house of a lady of position.

As the company was very numerous, the air became stiflingly hot, and caused the unfortunate girl to faint suddenly. The whole room was at once in a turmoil; they unfastened the bodice of her dress, in order to give her more air, and all at once two of the daintiest wax breasts fell to the ground from out of the gauze material of the bodice. The ladies screamed, and I do not doubt were secretly delighted at this public discovery. It can be imagined better than described, how great was the astonishment of the poor deceived bridegroom, who had doubtless often been bewitched by the charms of the alabaster bosom of his beloved. His love for the deceitful woman at once changed to the deepest scorn; the unfortunate girl was the object of general ridicule, and she lost at one and the same time her lover, admiration and esteem of her acquaintances.'

Towards the end of the nineteenth century the fashion for breast rings became popular in England. In a letter to a magazine one of the advocates of nipple-piercing talks about the 'operation':

"For a long time I could not understand why I should consent to such a painful operation without sufficient reason. I soon however came to the conclusion that many ladies are ready to bear the passing pain for the sake of love; I found that the breasts of the ladies who wore rings were incomparably rounder and fuller

36. Ladies under five feet might leave the hairdresser over seven feet tall.

37. The hem would often measure over twelve feet.

developed than those who did not. My doubts were now at an end. Although I am not naturally poorly-built, I had always wished for a really voluptuous bust with a slim figure, partly because I liked it for its own sake and also because it would be very advantageous to me in my profession. So I had my nipples pierced, and when the wounds were healed, I had rings inserted. They are naturally not especially costly or jewelled, but I am already quite satisfied with my shiny gold ones. With regard to the experience of wearing these rings, I can only say they are not in the least uncomfortable or painful. On the contrary, the slight rubbing and slipping of the rings causes in me an extremely agreeable titillating feeling, and all my colleagues to whom I have spoken on this subject have confirmed my opinion'.

Instead of rings small chains would often be fastened from breast to breast, with probably the most ostentatious being worn by an actress at the Gaiety theatre. This consisted of a pearly chain with a bow at each end.

38. A cock and hen party where both sexes would display their best clothes.

Throughout history new fashions have been ridiculed by the establishment before finally being accepted and often adopted by their critics. In 1875 "Queen" commented on the 'new' woman:

'The poor girls try to dress in a way which they fondly believe to be artistic, and end in looking like rag dolls. They tie the refuse of Cairo round their waists and wisps of strange fabrics round their necks. Peacocks' feathers eye us from unaccountable situations, and frills of old lace so dirty as to be almost nasty garnish throats which would look much better in clean linen collars.'

A criticism of 'the girl of the period' was published five years earlier:

Her cheeks are painted Babylon red,
With a chignon tall she adorned her head,
Of her bosom the padding's the total sum,
And she wears a bustle instead of a bum.

The pink of fashion, if too soon you call,
You'll find half dressed and not washed at all,
With a bottle of gin (false pride she disregards)
Telling fortunes in the kitchen with a dirty pack of cards.

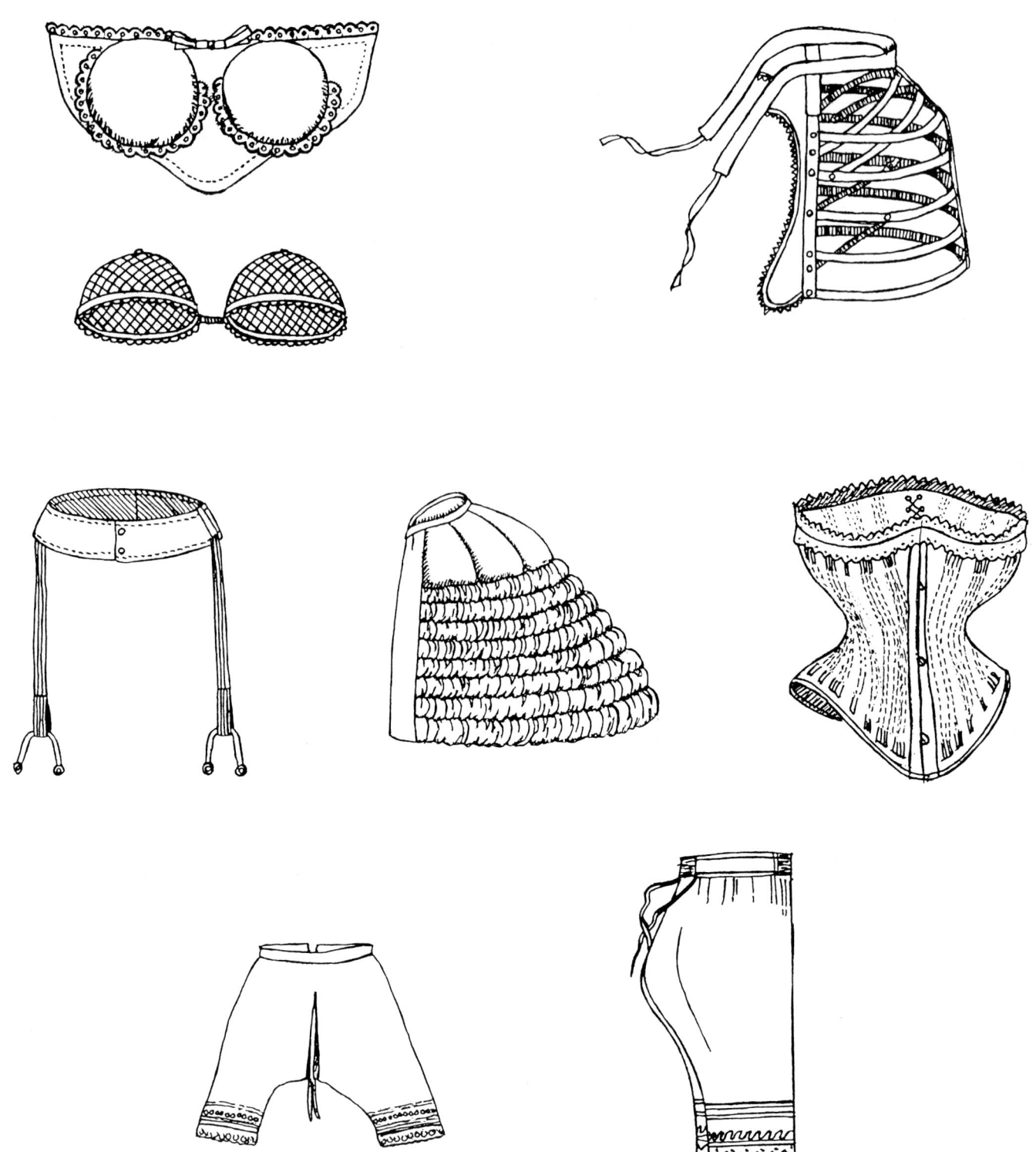

39. A selection of ladies' underwear, mostly from the nineteenth century.

When women started wearing drawers they were made of flannel, angola, calico and stocking-web. In the 1860's a wide choice of colours became available with magenta proving the most popular. A new style of underwear combining drawers and chemise became popular in the next decade, with the preferred hues now being pink and cream. They proved to be impractical and the 1870's closed with more prosperous women wearing chamois leather combinations as well as normal underclothes. The 'Englishwoman's Domestic Magazine' commented on the fashion for making personalised underwear:

'A young lady spent a month in hemstitching and embroidering a garment which it was scarcely possible that any other human being, except her laundress, would ever see.'

Lower income groups tried to follow the fashion of the day and maids would make their bustles from large numbers of kitchen dusters.

To improve their figure throughout the nineteenth century, corsets of different shapes and sizes were tightened around all forms of female flesh. At the start of the century half-inch-thick leather was used in their manufacture. Tight lacing led to the breasts being forced up until they were almost touching the chin and often caused serious injury to the liver. Of course the biggest danger was to the unborn child, though many mothers-to-be in the name of vanity ignored warnings and some even wore their corsets throughout the process of giving birth.

MALE FASHION; PRETTY FELLOWS, PERIWIGS AND PADDED UNDERHOSE

40. The Dandy in his favourite position — in front of the mirror.

There were many vain and dedicated followers of fashion amongst the capital's male population.

As long ago as Chaucer's days men were sporting close fitting hose which emphasised the buttocks and genital regions and the great storyteller noted that 'the buttocks behind' looked 'as if they were the hinder part of a sheape in the ful of the mone!'

A kind of exterior jockstrap was all the rage in Henry VIII's times. Known as a genital shield it was often padded to give a false impression of what might lie beneath. Hottenroth informs us:

> 'Hose were largely worn slit up their whole length and lined with padded underhose of another colour. They were bound with horizontal coloured stripes of material, short distances apart, or decorated in some other way with brightly-coloured strips of material inset. Thus fashioned the hose were called "trusses". The "genital shield," padded and slit was put on to a three-cornered flap, and though the "trusses" were nearly covered by coat flaps, could always be seen between the latter'.

In Elizabethan times the fashion conscious took to stuffing their hose with rags, feathers and other materials, causing special seats to be provided for them at public plays.

By the eighteenth century the dandies' dress was becoming more and more outrageous. They were to be seen parading in very tight gaily-checked jackets, waistcoats and breeches and became know by a variety of nicknames including; Maccaronis, Pretty Fellows, Bloods, Tulips, Fops, Swells, Sparks and of course Dandies.

They would parade self-consciously around town with large, tasselled walking sticks and red-heeled shoes. On their heads they would probably wear large knots of false hair topped by a miniature hat. When the fashion for wearing flesh-coloured tights was at its peak the dandies would parade through St. James's Park in very little else.

Schutz observed:

> "The suits were purposely made exceptionally tight so as to give more effect to the flesh colouring. This object was attained, as from a distance I really thought some inmates of Bedlam had escaped from their keepers and had put on only shoes and coats, leaving the rest of their bodies uncovered.

Wigs were going out of fashion towards the end of the eighteenth century. At the start the whole of Europe had been raided in the quest for hair and some went as far as the knee with just the eyes visible. For practical reasons they became shorter and the German observer of the British way of life, Archenoltz, comments:

> "The men resemble the women now more than in any other period. They wear their hair long and curled, sprinkled with flour and smelling of scent; they thicken it with borrowed curls."

There was a penchant for curls and in the barber's shop four people would be employed at the same time, three holding the hair in place whilst the fourth applied the hot irons.

Expensive wigs were too valuable to be thrown away and were passed on in the following manner. First it was left by will to son or heir; next it was given to the coachman; then with alterations to the gardener; then it went to the second-hand people in Monmouth Street, whence it continued a downward course until it finally entered upon its last career of usefulness in a shoeblack's box. The wig had come full circle as it was not uncommon for dandies to have their shoes cleaned more than ten times per day.

There was a sixpenny lucky-dip for wigs in Rosemary Lane, due to their becoming unfashionable. If a man still wanted a wig he would pay his sixpence and fetch up a new hairpiece. Sometimes he would get a good one; more often than not a grubby ill-fitting wig suitable only for the shoe-black. Men started wearing their hair powdered and tied back with black silk ribbon. This fashion was not without its practical problems as powder would often fall from the hair and help flavour the soup.

A visit to "a Pretty Fellow's Dressing-Room" by a contributor to the 'Connoisseur' could best help us visualise the dandy's appearance:

> "I was accordingly shown into a neat little chamber, hung round with Indian paper, and adorned with several little images of Pagods and Bramins, and vessels of Chelsea China, in which were set various-coloured sprigs of artificial flowers. But the toilet most excited my admiration, where I found everything was intended to be agreeable to the Chinese taste. A looking-glass, enclosed in a whimsical frame of Chinese paling, stood upon a Japan table, over which was spread a coverlid of the finest chintz. I could not but observe a number of boxes of different sizes, which were all of them Japan, and lay regularly disposed on the table. I had the curiosity to examine the contents of several; in one I found lip-salve, in another a roll of pig-tail, and in another the ladies' black sticking-plaster; but the last which I opened very much surprised me, as I saw nothing in it but a number of little pills. I likewise remarked, on one part of the table, a tooth-brush and sponge, with a pot of Delescot's opiate; and on the other side, water for the eyes. In the middle stood a bottle of Eau de Luce, and a roll of perfumed pomatum. Almond pastes, powder-puffs, hair-combs, brushes, nippers and the like, made up the rest of the fantastick equipage. But among other whimsies I could not conceive for what use a very small ivory comb could be designed, till the valet informed me that it was a comb for the eyebrows."

If the reporter had gone on to examine a dandy's wardrobe he might have discovered the following vestments listed by one of the swells:

> "My wardrobe consisted of five fashionable coats full mounted, two of which were plain, one of cut velvet, one trimmed with gold, and another with silver lace; two frocks, one of white drab with large plate buttons the other of blue with gold binding; one waistcoat of gold brocade, one of blue satin, embroidered with silver, one of green silk trimmed with broad figured gold lace, one of black silk with fringes . . ."

The list continues with three dozen ruffled shirts, silk handkerchiefs etc.

40a. Ernest Boulton was often seen around the capital in drag (Essex archives).

MEN IN PETTICOATS

In 1870 sexual relations between homosexuals was referred to, in legal jargon, as 'the abominable act' with participants liable to a prison sentence of more than ten years.

Transvestitism was a hobby almost exclusively carried out in front of mirrors behind locked doors.

The arrest of William Park and Ernest Boulton, and the lengthy press reports of their behaviour - both in the Victorian equivalents of tabloids and indeed in *The Times* - guaranteed that their trial would become one of the most discussed of the 1870's.

A police hearing to determine whether the men had a charge to answer began in the late Spring of 1870. Over the following two months the court was full to overflowing with a noisy, disruptive mob of *'a class of person very superior to the ordinary visitors to be seen at Bow-street'*.

The two men, both in their early twenties, were initially charged under the vagrancy act with frequenting. This was a very common charge for the times. What led to the courtroom being stuffed with spectators every day was the fact that the pair were apprehended in women's clothes.

Park and Boulton were arrested at the Strand Theatre following prolonged observation by the police. From their private box the two men in drag (a term used at this time) would smile and nod to the men in the stalls. They were also seen to play games and flick ash from their cigarettes into the gas. One of the suspects went into the ladies cloakroom to ask for some fallen lace to be pinned up. Neither wore wedding rings but both sported single rings. Following their arrest the two were held overnight in the cells, and, to the delight of the large crowd who had gathered, appeared in court the next day in the same costumes in which they had been arrested.

'In the dock Boulton wore a cherry-coloured evening silk dress trimmed with white lace: his arms were bare and he had on bracelets. He wore a wig and a plaited chignon. Park's costume consisted of a dark green satin dress, low necked, trimmed with black lace of which material he also had a shawl round his shoulders. His hair was flaxen and in curls. He had a pair of white kid gloves.'

Both men were remanded and police sent to search their rooms. These were bedecked with female clothes and accoutrements estimated to be worth over £200. These included: curling irons; sun-shades; six pair of stays; one low crossover; two tulle falls; chemisettes; garters; drawers; five boxes of violet powder; one bloom of roses [rouge]; silk stockings; eight pairs of gloves; artificial flowers and a great quantity of wadding used apparently for padding. There was also a small bottle of chloroform which today might appear suspicious but in Victorian times was used to counteract the ravages of toothache.

There were also large numbers of letters many of an intimate nature. Boulton would answer to the name of Stella and Park, Jane. One letter signed by John ended:

40b. Frederick Park answered to the name of Jane. He was charged with conspiring to incite others to commit an abominable offence (Essex archives).

"Probably it is better that I should stay and love and dream of you. But the thought of you, Louis and Autonious in one is ravishing."

Police had to decide whether the two men, who had appeared on the stage in drag were walking the street 'for a lark' as they said or for a more sinister reason.

A second far more serious charge was added: 'conspiring to incite others to commit an abominable offence.'

More correspondence was produced in evidence with The Times reporting:

"During reading of letters the audience in the body of the court appeared to be exceedingly amused, and the prisoners themselves smiled occasionally. Certain expressions of endearment addressed by one man to another caused such an outburst of laughter that Mr Poland (for the prosecution) rose and begged that such unseemly demonstrations might be checked."

A large number of witnesses as to the men's behaviour came forward to testify. A John Reeves said that he had seen them in Soho, dressed as women 'looking over their shoulders to entice men'. He had also seen them as males with low shirts, their faces painted and necks powdered..

A beadle stated that he had heard Boulton make noises with his mouth 'as women would to entice men. Boulton had shown him little respect calling him 'a sweet little dear'. Men who had kissed Boulton believing him to be a woman were produced and there were accusations that the accused were regulars at the Alhambra casino in Holborn, Burlington Arcade and even watched the boat race in drag. They would often be seen 'behaving stupidly, giggling and chirruping to each other, touching one another on the chin etc.'

A police surgeon took the stand and made some damning and rather unscientific comments, even for the 1870's. The accused were said to be suffering from a 'disease'. He added that with both men the 'criminal offence with which they had been charged had been committed time and time again.' He was effectively saying that both Park and Boulton had often participated in anal intercourse, though what evidence he had, only he knew. The Times 'protected' its readers from the more intimate details of the case. A doctor called by the defence found them perfectly normal. When it was decided that the case should be tried Park was visibly shocked protesting:

'I am innocent even of the thought of such a charge' to which Boulton added: *'I say the same.'*

The trial one year later lasted over a week and went over the same ground. The jury took one hour before acquitting them of the most serious charge. Instantaneous loud applause echoed through the courtroom. Boulton and Park were bound over to keep the peace for their offence 'against public morals and common decency.'

40c. The two men were arrested at the Strand Theatre. They appeared in court in women's clothes the following morning.

'AND THEN THE LOVER'

41. Love. Its beginning

its end.

CHOOSING A WIFE; 'GET TO SEE HER AT WORK UPON A MUTTON-CHOP'

One of the motives behind some of the outrageous fashions may have been to attract members of the opposite sex. In the early part of the nineteenth century William Cobbett advised young men to examine their chosen ones as they would a horse. His main recommendations however seemed to concern their housekeeping abilities:

> "Look a little at the labours of the teeth, for these correspond with those of the other members of the body and with the operations of the mind. 'Quick at meals, quick at work' is a saying as old as the hills. Never mind the pieces of needlework, the tambouring, the maps of the world made by her needle. Get to see her at work upon a mutton-chop or a bit of bread and cheese and if she deal quickly with these, you have a pretty good security for that activity, that stirring industry, without which a wife is a burden instead of a help. And as to love, it cannot live for more than a month or two (in the breast of a man of spirit) towards a lazy woman. Another mark of industry is a quick step and the eye kept steadily in the same direction while the feet are going, so much the better, for these discover earnestness to arrive at the intended point. I do not like, and I never liked, young, sauntering, soft-stepped girls who move as if they were perfectly indifferent to the result."

Advice and encouragement to married couples has always been available from those more experienced in the ways of the world. There was a remarkable openness towards the end of the seventeenth century with a Mrs. Behn offering her advice to women who have not conceived within the first three months of wedded life.

The woman whose advice to husbands after their wedding day was 'Those snow-white breasts, which before you durst scarce touch with your little finger you may now, without asking leave, grasp by whole handfuls' was more at home dealing with women's problems:

> 'She enquires very earnestly amongst her acquaintance what caresses they receive from their husbands; and most shamelessly relates what had passed between her and her husband, twixt the curtains or under the Rose; which she doth to that purpose that she may hear whether her husband understand his work well and whether he doth it well and oft enough; and also whether he be fully fit for the employ etc.'

If the man is 'not up to it' Mrs. Behn recommends oysters, eggs, coxcombs and the drinking of chocolate. If these remedies fail to have any effect on the husband the physical approach was recommended:

> 'I would many times myself by dallying with him and some other pretty Wanton postures, try to provoke him to it; whereby he should surely know that it was neither your coolness nor want of desire that might be blamed in it but rather always confess that you had sufficiently done your indeavour!'

ADVICE FOR THOSE WHO HAVE 'PLUKT TOO OFTEN FROM THE ROSE-TREE'

If the husband has 'Plukt too often from the Rose-tree' the following remedies are advocated: duck eggs, red cabbage with fat meat, old hens beaten to pieces, sweetbreads, coxcombs, sheep and goats' milk boiled with rice, calves and pigeons' brains with nutmegs grated in them and moderate quantities of Rhenish wine.

Doctor Graham's Temple of Health' furnished at a cost of £60,000 in the late 1700's was the destination of rich couples who had trouble conceiving. Transparent glass of every hue and the rarest perfumes would help to gently awaken desire and the couple would have to follow the instructions of the treatises on health. This was written to remove sterility from one sex and impotence from the other. The utmost attendance should be paid to cleanliness and a moderation in the sacrifices to Hymen (don't try too often). Retiring and rising early were also recommended and the light of the moon not be excluded by curtains. Married couples were advised to sing, music softening the minds of a happy couple, their bodies and souls uniting and their existence melting into a single being. The couples should raise themselves above this world and become inhabitants of a superior region. And now the advice that under no circumstances must be ignored. The couple should drink the divine balm, the secret concoction yours for the bargain price of one guinea!

And yes, ladies and gentlemen, for the night of your lives for the knockdown price of £50 you may spend the night on the most luxurious bed in London. It rests on transparent columns; bedclothes perfumed with the most costly essences of Arabia. The coverings are of purple and the curtains celestial blue. Make love to the melodious sounds of harmonica, the soft sounds of the flute and harmonious notes on the organ accompanied by an agreeable voice.

The temple was shut in 1784 and all goods sold.

A strange proposal was made at the church door by the bridegroom minutes before he was to be married. It was countered by the kind of quick-witted reply young street-wise London lasses were famous for:

"Dearest, during our courtship I have told you most of my mind, but I have not told you the whole. When we are married I shall insist upon three things."

"What are they?" replied the soon-to-be-wed young lady.

"In the first place I shall sleep alone, I shall eat alone and find fault where there is no occasion. Can you submit to those conditions?"

The reply was instantaneous:

"Oh, yes sir, very easily, for if you sleep alone I shall not; if you eat alone, I shall eat first; and as to your finding fault without occasion, that I think, may be prevented, for I shall take care you shall never want occasion!"

Greedy parents were not above 'selling' their daughters to rich sugar-daddies during Elizabethan times. Dekker in 'The Seven Deadly Sins of London' accuses some parents of showing more interest in the matching of their horses than a suitable matching for their children — it would not be uncommon to find a couple similar to those quoted at the aisle:

'He into whose bosum three-score winters have thrust their frozen fingers, if he be rich (though his breath be ranker than a muck-hill, his body more dry than a mummy, and his mind more lame than ignorance itself) shall have offered unto him (but it is offered as a sacrifice) the tender bosom of a virgin, upon whose forehead was never written sixteen years; if she refuse this living death (for less than a death it cannot be unto her) she is threatened to be left an out-cast, cursed for disobedience, railed at daily, and reviled hourly; to save herself from which baseness she desperately runs into a bondage, and goes to church to be married, as if she went to be buried . . .'

Who can resist the lonely hearts column of the local newspaper or magazine? Whatever one's age, sex or marital status they are compulsory reading for the browser. Although teenagers of every generation feel they invented sex, the more one reads on the subject the more one realises it has all been done before. The following extracts were printed towards the end of the 1700's. The bluntness of the advertising is just creeping back to today's magazines.

ON THE ROAD.—A GLIMPSE INTO OTHER PEOPLE'S TRAPS AS SKETCHED FROM THE TOP OF OUR DRAG.

42. In olden days a glimpse of stocking.

Isaac Cruikshank. PEEPERS IN BOND STREET, OR THE CAUSE OF THE LOUNGE! April 1793.

43. Peepers in Bond Street.

In 1791 a man was looking for a woman who:

> "Is well developed and full of grace in her person; more a beautifully made woman than a pretty one; good teeth, soft lips, agreeable breath; the colour of her eyes immaterial; further a firm and white bosum; affectionate and well educated but not witty..."
>
> If there is such a person, a gentleman 56 years old but vigorous and strong, is determined to marry her, however small her fortune may be. He possesses an income of £800 a year and is ready to make a preliminary settlement on her of £100. But she must agree to live entirely in the country, to love the husband of her choice with all her heart, and withal she must not be more than seven years older or fourteen years younger than I am.

An ad from Bristol in 1795:

> 'A gentleman needs a companion to journey with him towards matrimony; his intention is to depart as swiftly as possible, to leave the main roads and highways and to stroll in the paths in the wood of love. His fellow-traveller must be healthy, not too fat because that would make the journey troublesome, and to while away the hours of the marriage state, the chattier the better.'

Another advertiser was seeking a partner with soft lips, expressive eyes, sweet breath, 'bosum full, plump, firm and white,' lively conversation, humane temper and 'to look as if she could feel delight where she wishes to give it.'

The 'Public Advertiser' and the 'Morning Chronicle' printed most of the ads and it was not uncommon for admirers from a distance to make their first communication via newspaper advertisements:

> 'If the beauteous Fair One who was in the front boxes at the play Romeo and Juliet last Wednesday night dressed in a pink satin gown with a work'd handkerchief on, and a black feather in her hair with bugles; also a black ribbon round her neck and a solitaire; has a soul capable of returning a most sincere and ardent love to one who thinks he had the honour of being taken notice of by her as he sat in the side box; let her with all the frankness of a Juliet appoint in the paper or any other when, how and where she will give her Romeo a meeting.'

It was almost impossible to approach chaperoned women and desperate lovestruck men once again had to resort to print:

> "A young lady who was at Vauxhall on Thursday night last in company with the gentlemen could not but observe a young gentleman in blue and a gold laced hat, who, being near her by the orchestra during the performance, especially the last song, gazed upon her with the utmost attention. He earnestly hopes (if unmarried) she will favour him with a line directed to A.D. at the bar of the Temple Exhange Coffee House, Temple Bar, to inform him whether fortune, family and character may not entitle him upon a further knowledge to hope an interest in her heart."

Women would also place similar ads:

> 'A gentleman with a Spencer Wig who marched in the first rank of the Volunteers last Tuesday was particularly taken notice of by a lady of easy fortune and the world says she has some small share of beauty. If the said Gentleman is single and is disposed to send a line direct to D.Z. at the Somerset Coffee House in the Strand intimating his name and place of abode; if upon inquiry the lady finds his character answerable to his outward appearance she will then appoint him a meeting.'

43

LOVE LETTERS STRAIGHT FROM THE HEART

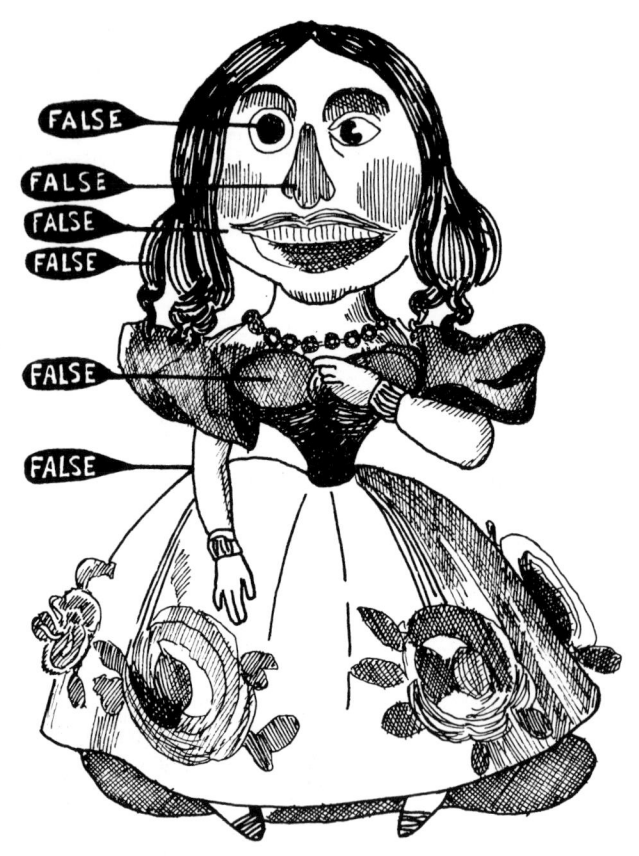

44. Cruel valentine.

In the early nineteenth century valentines fitted into one of three categories — sentimental, silly and nasty. The first category were similar to today's and might have hair, feathers, fur or ribbons attached and be scented with perfume. The silly and nasty cards would be sent to old maids or anybody with a physical or mental problem. There was even a book published with insulting verses wishing people disgrace, death and damnation.

A fairly mild form is quoted below, though one may imagine the distress it may have caused:

> *If the devil step'd, old lady, from his regions just below,*
> *He couldn't find a picture like the one before me now:*
> *No doubt you know the gentleman, a sable one is he,*
> *And he's said to be Papa of all the lies that yet might be.*
> *Your eyes are false, your nose is false, and falser still your tongue.*
> *Your breast is false, your heart is false, as ever poet sung;*
> *And if disgust did not prevail, upon my present will,*
> *I could speak of something villainous, and yet more filthy still.*

Another means of correspondence was of course the love letter.

It is not uncommon for young boys to fall for the charms of an older woman. The love of the young Count de la Rochefoucauld for the forty-five year old mother of several children, Lady Cavendish, has been remembered for one reason more than any other. Twelve of the Count's love letters occupy the last twenty-six pages of one of England's most erotic books.

Apparently the replies from the lady were even more scandalous though these were never read other than by the young man. The contents of the Count's letters led to the Lady's disgrace and divorce:

> "*I have never kissed another woman, and whatever misfortune may befall it will always be an indescribable happiness for me to remember that I lost my innocence through your enchanting caresses. This is perhaps the greatest happiness and the one consolation in my life — and will remain so. But before God, it is a great happiness and my delight such as cannot be found again on earth. I do not believe that he who took your innocence was as pure as I was, and if there is a greater joy than that which I know, I promise you never to seek or experience it, though I do not ask the same of you. I do not wish to hear other women spoken of: even to look at them disgusts me. You know it, and you know too that nothing in you disgusts me, but that everything that is you enchants me, and I love and worship it all. It is a kind of madness and you know it; for when you are kind you give me, at least in writing, the idea of that which you would not do, if you harboured the least doubt about it . . . As much as the odour of woman is repugnant to me in general, the more do I like it in you. I beg of you to preserve that intoxicating perfume; but you are too clean, you wash yourself too much. I have often told you so in vain. When you will be quite my own I shall forbid you to do it too often, at most, once a day, my tongue and my saliva will do the rest.*"

45. Some greetings were sincere.

SIN IN VICTORIAN LONDON

KEY

1. One of the capital's leading flagellation establishments was in Circus Road and very popular with Swinburne.
2. Amy Johnson, alias Hope, alias Scott, one of the leading demi-mondaines of the 1850s lived in Connaught Terrace.
3. York Street was the home of a brothel with just one customer, an aged duke.
4. Victorian striptease or tableaux vivants was popular in New Road.
5. The famous prostitute Mrs. Billings lived over an auctioneers in Charlotte Street and available to the highest bidder.
6. Bedford Square was the home of the 'yellow book' whose scandalous drawings and daring articles attacked the hypocrisy of the 1890s.
7. Madame Audrey's 'introducing house' in Church Street, Soho.
8. A notorious promenade for the most expensive prostitutes was to be found in the Empire Theatre of Varieties.
9. Great Windmill Street, the Casino was a popular rendezvous for prostitutes.
10. Willis's in Brewer Street, the dancing was raunchy with many couples getting carried away.
11. The 'Juliets of a night' especially the under-fifteens could be found parading between Piccadilly Circus and Waterloo Steps.
12. Some of the most expensive street-walkers were to be found in the Haymarket.
13. Burlington Arcade offered warmth and accommodation at a price to the prostitutes in winter. They would come to an arrangement with shopkeepers and beadles.
14. The shoes in the window in Jermyn Street would inform those in the know that Mrs. Clarke, a famous courtesan of the 50s, was open for business.
15. Another 'introducing house'. This one in Bury Street by Madame Landeau.
16. Piccadilly. At the age of almost eighty, the British Prime Minister who lived here was cited in a divorce case. A popular joke that did the rounds at that time asked about the relationship between Palmerston and a former governess Margaret O'Kane; 'while the lady was certainly Kane, was Palmerston Abel?'

46.

47.

17. Chesterfield Street, home of the 'last great Victorian courtesan,' Catherine Walters or Skittles as she was more popularly known. She was rumoured to have leaders of political parties and a member of the Royal family amongst her 'friends'.
18. The three Miss Butterworths were the main attraction at the Lowther Rooms. One of the most popular venues for theatre whores.
19. The Feathers in Hart Street, one of the many night-houses.
20. The Ship; 'market porters, doxies, high and low pads.'
21. The Seven Dials, an area where many a smutty song has become popular.
22. The Almonary was pulled down from this site as it was deemed to be a centre of vice.
23. Wilton Crescent, home of the reformed prostitute Laura Bell. In her early years she was presented with a gift of £250,000 by Prince Jung Bahadoor of Nepal. Later in life Laura organised prayer meetings and sought to help the local prostitutes.

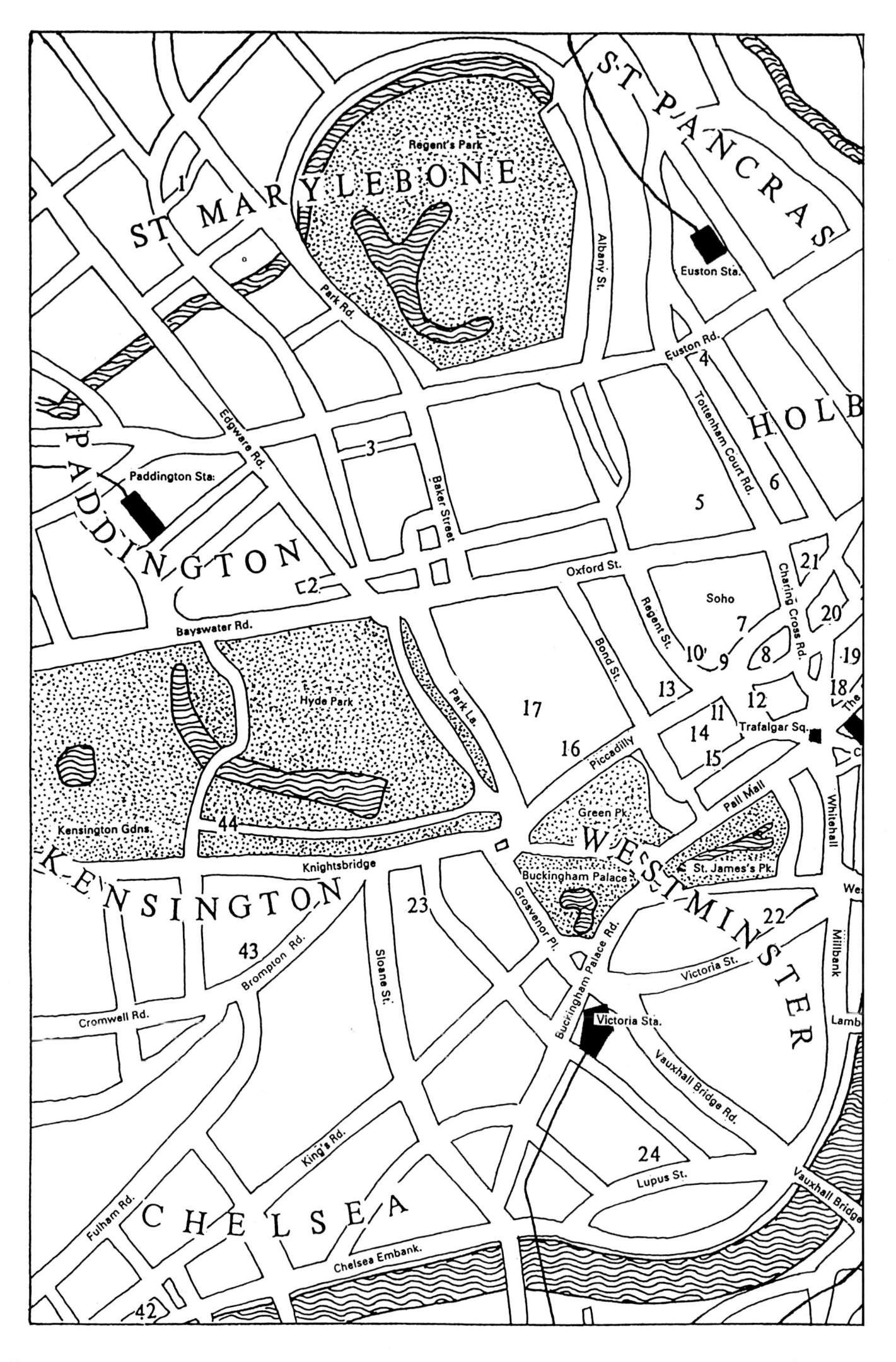

St Marylebone / Paddington / Westminster / Kensington / Chelsea

Labels visible on map:

- ST. PANCRAS
- ST. MARYLEBONE
- Regent's Park
- Euston Sta.
- Euston Rd.
- HOLB(ORN)
- Park Rd.
- Albany St.
- Tottenham Court Rd.
- Edgware Rd.
- PADDINGTON
- Paddington Sta.
- Baker Street
- Oxford St.
- Charing Cross Rd.
- Soho
- Bayswater Rd.
- Regent St.
- Bond St.
- Trafalgar Sq.
- Hyde Park
- Park La.
- Piccadilly
- Kensington Gdns.
- Green Pk.
- Pall Mall
- St. James's Pk.
- Whitehall
- KENSINGTON
- Knightsbridge
- Buckingham Palace
- WESTMINSTER
- Brompton Rd.
- Sloane St.
- Grosvenor Pl.
- Victoria St.
- Millbank
- Cromwell Rd.
- Buckingham Palace Rd.
- Victoria Sta.
- Vauxhall Bridge Rd.
- Lamb(eth)
- King's Rd.
- Fulham Rd.
- Lupus St.
- Vauxhall Bridge
- CHELSEA
- Chelsea Embank.

Numbered locations: 1, 2, 3, 4, 5, 6, 7, 8, 9, 10, 11, 12, 13, 14, 15, 16, 17, 18, 19, 20, 21, 22, 23, 24, 42, 43, 44

SIN MAP OF LONDON IN VICTORIAN TIMES

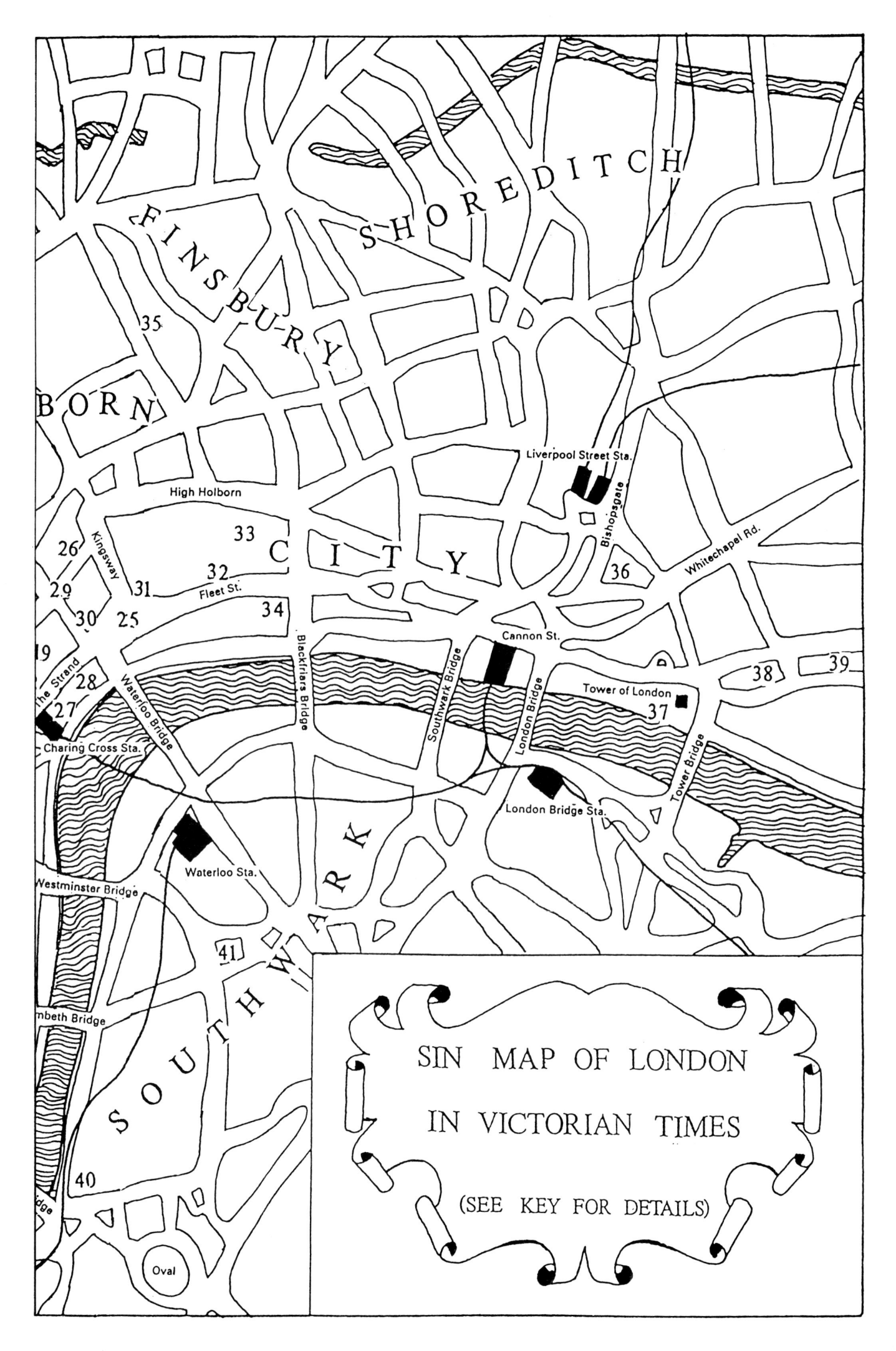

(SEE KEY FOR DETAILS)

24. M.P.s had their privileges. There was an introducing house in Lupus Street catering for the needs of the elected members.
25. The centre of the pornography trade in Holywell Street.
26. Drury Lane, the lower end of the female flesh market.
27. The Shades, a celebrated underground venue.
28. The Coal Hole, a famous Bohemian song-and-supper resort where 'a smart smutty song may occasionally be heard.'
29. The Union in Bow Street; bawdy ballads and half-naked dancers were the order of the day.
30. The Albert Saloon. Another renowned meeting-place.
31. 'Scarcely better than a brothel' was the contemporary assessment of The White Lion in Wych Street.
32. The Haunch of Venison in Bell Yard, Fleet Street, a famous haunt for abandoned women.
33. The Three Tuns on Fetter Lane, more bawdy ballads. 'The songs sung are of the beastly description.'
34. One of the roughest pubs in the capital. The Twelve Bells, Bridle Lane.
35. 'One of the most prolific publishers of filthy books,' William Dugdale, died in the Clerkenwell House of Correction.

49. Mabel Gray, a high class prostitute.

36. The Cross Keys, Gracechurch Street. 'Private rooms can be had here either by day or night; the charge for a sleeping room for self and lady is 4s, but for a short visit the mere calling for wine is deemed sufficient.'
37. One of the Cock-and-hen clubs. The Nag's Head, Tower Hill.
38. Dock Street. Location of one of the many child brothels. This one run by Katherine Keeley.
39. Another Child brothel in Betts Street, a Mrs. Maxwell was the resident Madam.
40. Vauxhall Gardens the fun place to be in the middle of the century. Fireworks, concerts, jugglers and tight-rope walkers were some of the attractions. Others were to be found behind the odd bench or tree.
41. The Surrey Theatre was off the beaten track and of great interest for the well-to-do gent seeking a little salacious excitement.
42. Cremorne Gardens. Respectable by day, the haunt of street-walkers by night. The Gardens were closed in the late 1870s.
43. The Prime Minister Gladstone pursuaded the inhabitant at number 36 to give up her wicked ways.
44. Rotten Row. The poser's playground. All the most famous courtesans could be spotted displaying their charms in ornate carriages in the middle years of the century.

50. Nellie Rousby. Often to be seen on Rotten Row.

51. Victoria was said to be fond of 'the Albert Cordial'.

A ROYAL MARRIAGE MADE IN HEAVEN

One of the most enduring romances of the nineteenth century was between a 'short and not well proportioned woman; her bust is somewhat fine; her mouth is imbecile in expression; her teeth are irregular but sound, and her hands are not white.'

The man 'is of the height of five feet ten inches; his figure is not well-proportioned; in walking he has a stoop.'

Only two years after her coronation Victoria fell head-over-heels in love with the young german, Prince Albert. He was three months younger than the Queen and had shown previously little interest in the opposite sex. For her part Victoria was immediately smitten. She confided in her diary:

> "It is with some emotion that I beheld Albert - who is beautiful. I embraced them both [Albert and his brother] and took them to Mamma... [He] was quite charming, and so excessively handsome, such beautiful blue eyes, and exquisite nose, and such a pretty mouth with delicate moustachios and slight but very light whiskers: a beautiful figure broad in the shoulders and fine waist: my heart is quite going..."

It was Victoria who proposed as Albert was later to relate to his grandmother:

> 'She declared to me in a genuine outburst of love and affection that I had gained her whole heart and would make her intensely happy if I would make her the sacrifice of sharing her life with her.'

The engagement was kept secret for a few days. Vicky asked Albert for a lock of his 'dear hair' and gave him her ring.

The besotted English Queen and her chosen German Prince played cards and held long conversations well into the night. It appears from Vicky's diary entries that she was counting the days to when she would no longer be a virgin Queen:

> "We embraced each other over and over again, and he was so kind, so affectionate. Oh! to feel I was, and am, loved by an Angel as Albert was too great a delight to describe! He is perfection, perfection in every way - in beauty - in everything...Oh! how I adore and love him I cannot say!!"

With the announcement of the wedding the British press wasted little time in trying to undermine the relationship. The love/hate affair between the press and Royal Family is far from being a late twentieth century phenomenon. They hated Albert almost with the same passion that Vicky loved him. He was referred to as the pauper Prince and was often mocked, the following four lines is a rather poor play on words about cards:

> "They say I'm a ninny
> and not worth a ginny
> But Vic, she declares
> I'm a trump"

Shortly after their plans were made public Albert had to return to the continent to settle his affairs. Vicky could barely entertain the thought that they would be parted. On November 14th 1839, Vicky gave her husband to be the kind of sending off he would never forget. She once again confided in her diary:

> "We kissed each other so often, and I leant on that dear soft cheek, fresh and pink as a rose...I gave Albert a last kiss... I cried much, felt wretched yet happy to think we should meet again so soon. Oh! how I love him, how intensely, how ardently. I cried and felt so sad."

Albert too must have wondered why he had waited so long to taste the pleasures of the opposite sex. He wrote to Vicky:

> "Your image fills my whole soul. Even in my dreams I never imagined that I should find so much love on earth."

Because of parliamentary business the honeymoon at Windsor was short but the couple wasted little time. The first evening was spent on the sofa, the newly-weds getting to know each other a little more intimately. The sheer joy of living runs through the Queen's reminiscences:

> "...he clasped me in his arms and we kissed each other again and again. His beauty, his sweetness and gentleness - really how can I ever be thankful enough to have such a husband."

Albert called her such tender names that she was 'in bliss beyond belief'. Despite their lack of experience the couple had few problems finding where everything fitted. Little Vicky was not one of the frigid 'have you finished yet?' variety of bed partner. She certainly did not just lie back and it's more likely that Germany rather than England was on her mind.

On the second day of married life Victoria noted in her diary:

> "When day dawned (for we did not sleep much) and I beheld that beautiful angelic face by my side, it was more than I can express. He does look so beautiful in his shirt only, with his beautiful throat seen."

A few weeks after the wedding the novelty had not worn off:

> "You cannot imagine how delightful it is to be married. I could not have dreamed that anyone could be so happy in the world a I am."

The pleasures of sexual intercourse made the Queen positively glow. She was blissfully happy between the sheets with the man she loved. Such a difference from the sombre photographs of her later years when she came across as a dumpy depressed matriarch.

Jokes and humour surrounded the couple from their wedding night onwards and every movement was observed and commented upon:

'She and Prince Albert were up very early on Tuesday morning, walking about, which is very contrary to their former habits. Strange that a bridal night should be so short; and I told Lady Palmerston that this was no way to provide us with a Prince of Wales.'

"So Albert goes with the Queen to Windsor after the ceremony."
"He'll go further before morning."
"How so?"
"Why, he'll go in at Bushy, past Virginia Water, on through Maidenhead and leave Staines behind."

There was a more subtle style of writing with the royal couple once again being the subjects of tongue-in cheek mockery:

'Thomas Bradley, the physiological phenomenon, is said to sleep for forty, fifty, and a hundred hours, without waking. When Prince Albert was told of the extraordinary circumstances, he expressed great surprise, and declared that there was a vast difference between the dormant faculties of poor Bradley and his little beloved Vic, who, he said, never slept more than an hour at a time, and who would no return again to sleep without he instantly rose, and gave Her Majesty what she is so dearly fond of viz. the Albert Cordial, which upon all occasions, immediately composes and stimulates Her Majesty to sleep.'

The couple would often be noticed whispering sweet nothings to each other in German and Albert helped his wife to dress and put on her stockings. Albert slept in white drawers, similar to the sleeping suit worn by babies. Both his feet and legs were enclosed. Vicky was described as warm and Albert cold, though whether this referred to their body temperature or passion is unclear. The couple seemed ideally matched and at their happiest in the privacy of the bedroom. Albert wrote to his brother:

"A married couple must be chained to one another, be inseparable, and they must live only one for another. I wish you could be here and see in us a couple united in love and unanimity."

The pair were certainly fast learners. Vicky noticed the tell-tale signs of pregnancy when experiencing morning

51a. A family group photograph taken two years before Albert's premature death.
From L to R: the Count of Flanders, Albert, Princess Alice, the Duke of Oporto, the Prince of Wales, Queen Victoria, King Leopold 1 of the Belgians.

sickness just one month after the wedding. As she was later to confide, the Queen enjoyed the making of her babies but positively detested their nine months in transit. Albert, for his part, was delighted at the prospect of becoming a father. He positively purred at the enlargement of his wife's breasts. Vicky was not so little any more.

Following a turbulent twelve hours the Queen gave birth on 21st November 1840.

When told that she had a daughter Vicky casually replied that it did not matter as the next child would be a Prince. The baby was christened Victoria Adelaide Mary Louisa and would in later life become the Queen's closest confident.

In the mid 1800s the menstrual cycle was not fully understood and couples wishing not to conceive were told not to have intercourse immediately after a period, but to wait for some two weeks! Not surprisingly Vicky fell again the following year. She and Albert barely spent a night apart, and apart from his leggings, barely spent the night together. Vicky rarely suffered from headaches and washed her hair during the day. Writing openly about sex the Queen observed:

> "Certainly it is unbounded happiness - if one has a husband one worships! It is a foretaste of heaven."

If sex was heaven then pregnancy was hell. Throughout her second confinement, Vicky was depressed and bad-tempered, often snapping at the man she worshiped. A third baby quickly followed and in total Victoria had to endure nine pregnancies and she was amongst the first women in the country to use anaesthetics when giving birth. She was also one of the lucky few prescribed cannabis to help alleviate period pains!

Shortly after the birth of her second daughter, Princess Alice in 1843, Albert returned to Germany following reports of the wayward undisciplined life his brother had been leading the past few years. In most marriages following the birth of three children the initial love and euphoria might have been expected to have worn a little thin, not so with the British Queen. She cried throughout the day of Albert's departure confiding:

> "I have never been away from him even for one night and the thought of such separation is quite dreadful."

Albert too was still closely attached and missed Vicky every day. He wrote in Germany:

> "How glad I should be to have my little wife beside me, that I might share my pleasure with her."

Following the birth of child number 4, Prince Alfred, the couple began to spend a good deal of their free time at Osborne House on the Isle of Wight. These were probably the Queen's happiest years (at least when she was not with child). Both Victoria and Albert delighted in the arts and would often make each other paintings, often nudes. They would both sing and play musical instruments and often read to each other. Victoria wrote in the mid 1840s that:

> "Without him everything loses its interest. It will always be a terrible pang for me to separate from him even for two days: and I pray God never to let me survive him."

In 1861, at the relatively young age of 42, Albert fell seriously ill. He could neither sleep nor keep down food. The medical men of the times believed him to be suffering from typhoid, it may well have been stomach cancer. As he writhed in agony his children read to him and sang german songs. Putting on a brave face Victoria would read to him from Walter Scott. In private she wept and prayed incessantly. With death approaching Vicky addressed her husband for the last time calling him by all the tender pet names she could conjure up before finally being led from the room.

Against his wishes a death mask of the Prince was taken. For years little Vicky slept with her dead husband's nightshirt held close to her body. She knelt every night at Albert's side of the bed before retiring to her own side. Victoria kept a cast of Albert's hand in her bedroom at all times. The routine in all households was to carry on as if Albert was still alive. Boiling water was produced every morning for his shave and the unused chamber pot withdrawn and emptied.

The Queen later confided in her daughter how much she missed the physical side of the relationship:

> "...at 42 all those earthly feelings must be crushed and the never quenched flame... burns within me and wears me out...I am alas not old - and my feelings are strong and warm; my love is ardent."

Victoria went into deep mourning and depression and was never the same person again. The young Queen's twenty odd years of marriage were without a doubt the happiest of her life. One can imagine how lonely her nights were as the Queen of England lay back and thought of Germany.

Not all royal marriages were as successful as that of Victoria and Albert.

AND ONE IN HELL

At the age of 14, Caroline Amelia Elizabeth of Brunswick was described as *'a lively, pretty child with light coloured hair hanging in curls on her neck, with rosebud lips from which it seemed that none but sweet words could flow, and always sweetly and modestly dressed.'*

Caroline had peaked early. By the age of 26, by royal standards, she had been left on the shelf. The flush of youth had long since passed, she neglected her personal hygiene and stories of her flirting and use of coarse language became the talk of the court. In short she *'swore like an ostler and smelt like a farmyard'*.

Back in England, the future King George 1V was leading an equally dissolute life.

At the age of 18 he *'drank hard, swore and passed every night in brothels'*. He had even conducted a secret illegal marriage with the assistance of an Anglican clergyman bailed from the Fleet prison. If news of the wedding had leaked out there may well have been rioting in the streets. Not for the fact that his bride, Maria Fitzherbert, was six years his senior but because she was a Roman Catholic.

By 1794 the Prince had run up a long list of gambling debts. Only if he was officially married could there be a significant increase in his allowance from the civil list. Now 32, and with serious financial difficulties, the spoilt Prince started looking for a suitor. His cousin, Caroline, whom he had never met, was free (and easy). George sent an aide to the continent to report back on the suitability of the German for the post of future Queen of England.

The man assigned to the job was Lord Malmesbury and his first impressions were far from satisfactory. At their first meeting the Lord made notes as to Caroline's personal hygiene:

'She neglects it sadly and is offensive from this neglect."

It appears that on the occasions she did wash, Caroline would only clean those areas not clothed i.e. her face and hands. A Madame Burke was charged to pass on the message later made famous in 'Lifebouy' adverts.

The following day Caroline appeared washed 'all over'. But old habits die hard, and if she washed herself a little more often this was not true of her clothes.

Lord Malmesbury was particularly scathing about her garments:

"I know she wore coarse petticoats, coarse shifts, and thread stockings and these never washed nor changed often enough."

Nonetheless the Lord believed she could adapt and the Prince's debts were crippling.

On Sunday 5th. April 1795 the two enfants terribles of their respective countries met on an irreversible form of blind date. To say they were both disappointed would be the understatement of the eighteenth century century.

Let's hear Lord Malmesbury's account of the fateful afternoon:

"I immediately notified the arrival to the King and Prince of Wales; the last came immediately. I, according to the established etiquette, introduced (no one else being in the room) the Princess Caroline to him. She very properly, in consequence of my saying it to her it was the right mode of proceeding, attempted to kneel to him.

He raised her (gracefully enough) and embraced her, said barely one word, turned round, returned to a distant part of the apartment and calling me to him said:

'Harris, I am not well: pray get me a glass of brandy.'

I said: 'Sir, had you better not have a glass of water?', upon which he, much out of humour, said with an oath, 'No, I will go directly to the Queen' and away he went.

The Princess, left during this short moment alone, was in a state of astonishment; and on my joining her said [in French] "My God, is the Prince always like that. I find him fat and nowhere near as good looking as his portrait.' '

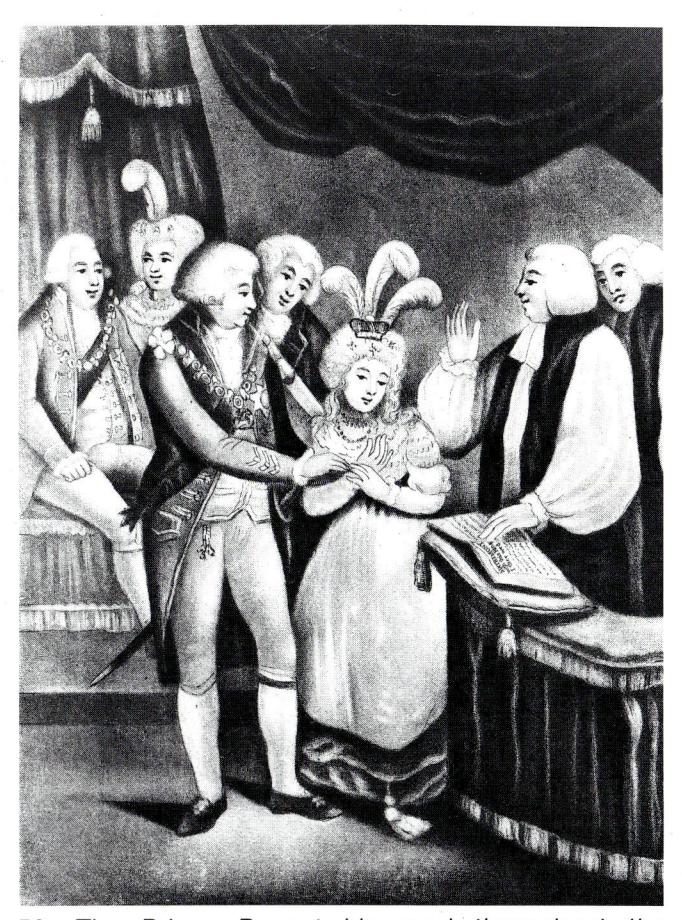

52. The Prince Regent hiccuped throughout the marriage ceremony.

Nonetheless, the Prince was committed to the marriage which he attended hiccuping continuously throughout the ceremony, due to his drunkenness. His behaviour did not improve afterwards as he ignored his wife and openly stepped out with other women. The future George IV often shut up his bride and surrounded her with spies. Although the couple produced a daughter one year after marriage, the Prince let it be known that they could no longer live as man and wife. Amongst the Prince's complaints were that Caroline ate raw onions, rarely bathed and changed her undergarments only infrequently. Caroline moved to Blackheath two years after her marriage and set up home in Montague House. Stories of infidelity soon got back to the Prince and even though he had a string of mistresses himself, when he heard of the decadent life being led by his wife, who had moved abroad, he ordered the house to be burnt down and ironically all that now remains is the sunken bath.

Caroline had gone into voluntary exile in 1814 and spent some time travelling in Europe, especially Italy. When the mad George III died in 1820 the Prince came to the throne and despite George's attempts to prevent her, Caroline returned to become Queen. The King had her brought before the House of Lords on a charge of infidelity with a certain Bergami and the divorce trial, the most famous in British history, lasted nearly three months.

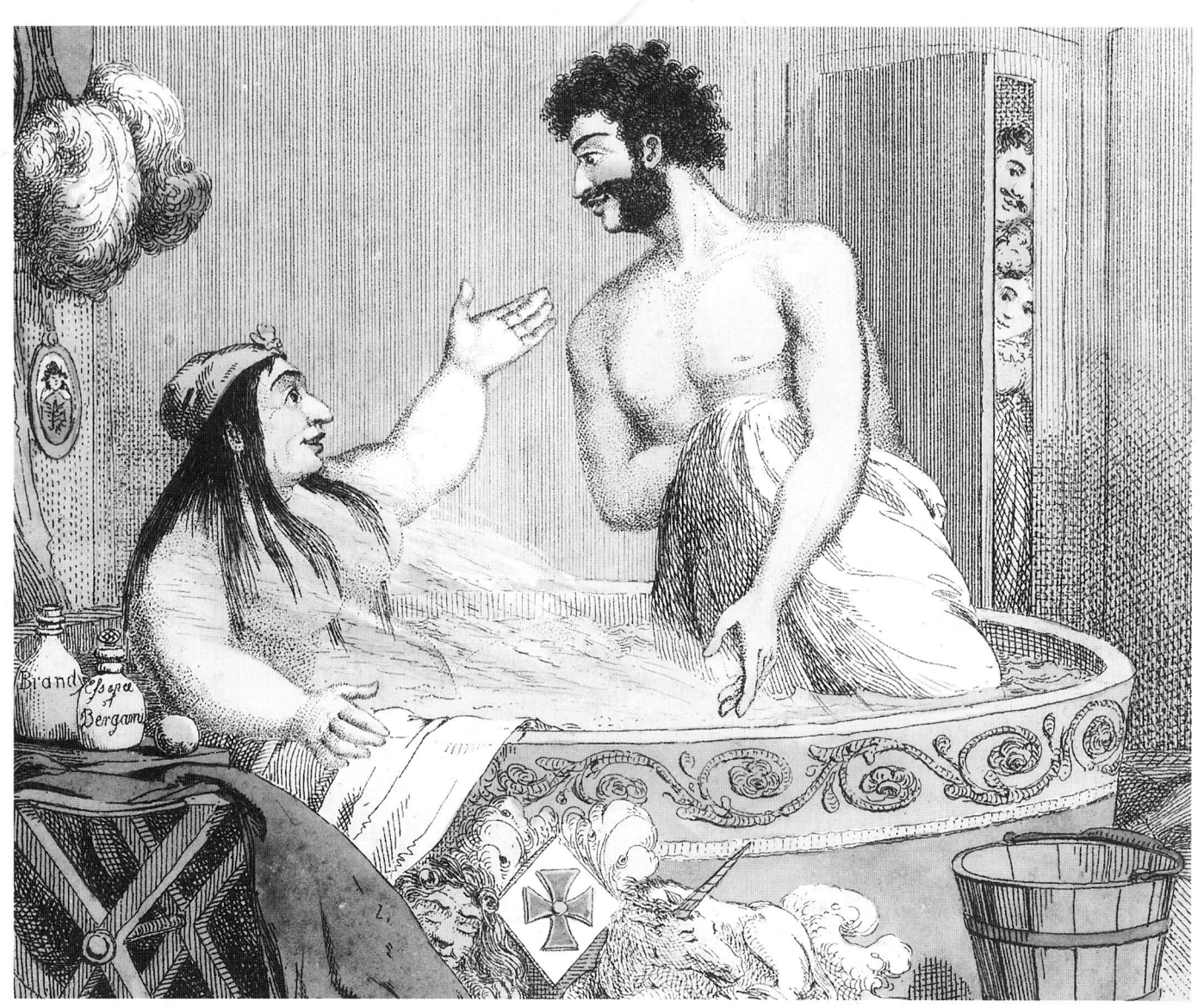

52a. It was rather ironic that a Queen not noted for her personal hygiene should be observed in flagrante in the bath. (© British Museum).

52b. The row between George and Caroline split the country (© British Museum).

Scores of foreign hotel-waiters and chambermaids were shipped to London to give evidence against the Queen, some of which we may present here:

> "Were you ever present when Bergami's bed was warmed?"
> "I was not there when the bed was warmed but I brought a hot-water bottle."
> "Did you see Bergami get out of bed to let it be warmed?"
> "Yes."
> "Was the Princess in the room at that time?"
> "Yes."

Another testimony followed:

> 'At Karlsruhe Her Majesty was one day found in Bergami's room; she was sitting upon his bed, and he was in bed with his arm around the neck of Her Majesty. She was surprised in this extraordinary situation by one of the femmes de chambre, who was going into the room by chance . . . in that bed was found a cloak, which her majesty was afterwards seen wearing; and in that bed, also, certain marks were also observed by one of the servants. These marks, without his saying anything further at present, would leave their lordships perhaps to infer that which he wished them to understand.'
>
> "What was the state of Bergami's dress at the time you saw him in the passage going towards the bedroom of Her Royal Highness?"
> "He was not dressed."
> "When you say he was not dressed, what do you mean; what had he on?"
> "He was not dressed at all."

Despite the damning testimonies of the witnesses the Queen was completely exonerated, thanks largely to the brilliant defence of Lord Brougham. The pit stood up and the men waved their hats, and the women their handkerchiefs, the cheering and acclamations lasting for several minutes.

Caroline died in 1821 of a bowel inflammation and thousands took to the streets to say a final farewell as the body was eventually taken back to the Continent via Romford and Harwich.

Her departure was in deep contrast to the rudeness experienced upon her arrival in London a quarter of a century earlier.

DIVORCE — 'FROM BED, BOARD AND MUTUAL COHABITATION'

The greatest divorce sensation of the eighteenth century was that of Mrs. Elizabeth Draper in 1771, related by Ivan Bloch in his book: 'A History of English Sexual Morals.'

She was the eldest of the ten children of a grocer named Hartnill, and married Richard Draper on 16th August 1764, being then no longer a virgin. She was a perfect example of English beauty and bewitched everybody with her loveliness. The first who could boast of her favours was a small negro in the service of her father. She was ten years old when he seduced her. At fifteen she married Mr. Draper, a rich merchant who was unfortunately impotent, but even had he been otherwise he would hardly have been able to prevent his wife's daily increasing love-mania from finding extravagant expression. When she was first married and living on Mr. Draper's estate in the country, she took intense pleasure in watching the mating of mares and stallions . . . Very soon after her first marriage she began to lead a dissolute life. Her first liaison was in 1766 with a coachman, Charles Russell; then she made an apprentice, William Penfold, her victim, who at the age of fifteen entered Mr. Draper's service in London an innocent country lad. Three weeks after his arrival, Mrs. Draper approached after dinner, kissed him, undressed him and then herself and seduced him. In court the obedient apprentice declared that he had to perform this service for his mistress twice a week. The virility of coachmen also appealed to her, as the postilion John Haylock enjoyed her favours at the same time. A maid, Sarah Eliot, asserted that after Haylock had visited Mrs. Draper the condition of the bed proved that adultery had been committed.

Meanwhile, Mrs. Draper's nymphomania had reached its height. Miss Rutt relates that she once surprised three young fellows in her room. Mary Allen, a servant, watched through a hole in the wall how her mistress sat with bare breasts in front of John Lancaster, a neighbouring landowner:

> 'Lancaster was taking liberties with her. At this time the boards on which she was standing, making a little noise, she heard Mrs. Draper say, somebody was coming; on which she retired into the next room, but soon returned and looked through again; they had then left the fireplace, but the bed being near the door, she plainly heard them on it, and heard it crack and make a noise as if persons were pressing upon it; she also heard them whisper upon the bed. She continued listening for some minutes, and believed that they were committing the crime of adultery together.'

One day a certain James Delegal was sitting in the theatre at Islington when he suddenly felt the lady next to him 'put her hand on his private parts' and try to attract him to her. It was Mrs. Draper, who this time, however, was not fortunate. As last witness the 17 year-old Edward Goode gave evidence. He came to London about the middle of 1770 and saw Mrs. Draper for the first time at dinner in her husband's house. At the table she trod on his foot and secretly pressed his hand. At first he thought it was a joke, but the very next day she enticed him into a room, where there was a bed, put her arms around his neck and confessed her love. He tore himself away and fled, while she shouted threats after him. On the following day she sent for him. She lay in bed; and stopping by the door he asked her what she wanted. She said come into bed with me; whereupon he immediately went away. A little later she came down to him dressed.

The following account was continued in French for some unknown reason, I have translated . . .

> "She rushed up and sat on my knees, mixes kisses with the most tender talk and runs her hand through my . . . chest, lifts up her skirt and asks me 'Do you want to?' And I committed the sin of adultery. The following day after dinner, with her husband at the bottom of the stairs she came and straddled me."

The young man pictures in lively colours how he and the apprentice Penfold shared the ceaseless favours of this Messalina; and how at last, driven by pangs of conscience, they revealed everything to the master of the house. This remarkably scandalous case ended in complete divorce.

THROUGH THE CHAMBER KEYHOLE

The trial of Captain Gambier at the Guildhall on 11th June 1757 would have had the courthouse overflowing with representatives from all levels of society. Everyone loved a juicy scandal and they were in for a treat from the testament of Admiral Knowles' chambermaid.

Captain Gambier was charged with "having criminal conversation with the wife of Admiral Knowles." Let's hear some of the testimony:

> "I went into my mistress's bed chamber, and, upon viewing my mistress's bed which I had made in the morning, I perceived the impression of the bodies of two persons, as though they had been amorously laying and tumbling thereon; and on the bolster of the bed my mistress had left her hat. I saw her afterwards without her hat; and her clothes and things were rumpled and tumbled, as is usual when men and women play together and hug, kiss and tumble one another . . .
>
> "My mistress would often pull off her stays against the usual time of the captain's coming: sit with him in every amorous posture imaginable; sometimes he would embrace her, sometimes with his hand round her waist, look at, and ogle her; and she would in return sigh, coo, and smile at him and often pat and stroke him; and then they would often go away, and be absent sometimes half an hour, sometimes two hours or more.
>
> "In my mistress's bed-chamber was a closet, and the closet was cleared and cleaned out and the captain went into the closet, and fitted himself to it, that in case of the sudden arrival of the admiral, the captain might hide himself there.
>
> "Curiosity led me two or three times to look through the key-hole of the chamber door. The first time I looked through I could very plainly see on one side of the bed, that side on which the captain lay, his shoes which were near the foot of the bed; just by stood a chair on which the captain's coat and waistcoat hung; the captain getting out of bed and going to put his clothes on, I came away from the door."
>
> Q. "This was the first time: pray what did you see the next time you looked through your mistress's door?"
>
> A. "I was going to tell you. It was the next morning; on a chair were hanging my mistress's gown and petticoat and on the bed-mat near the chair I saw one of my lady's white stockings, and a garter with a silver buckle. It being fine summer weather and the sun shining very bright, I saw my mistress get out of bed, go to the window, draw back the curtains and then return back and go into bed again."
>
> Q. "This was the second time, did you ever after look through the door?"
>
> A. "I came to the door about half an hour after four o'clock in the morning. The captain and my lady were laughing, playing, talking; they talked partly in English and partly in French. The defendant got out of the bed, walked round the foot of the bed, made use of something that was on my lady's side of the bed, and then he jumped into bed on the same side, and soon after I believe both parties were as happy in the mutual enjoyment of one another as they were on the 23rd day of April in the governor's own house in Jamaica."

The maid continued:

> "when my lady received the captain at home, she would do it in a loose dress, without her stays: and sometimes they would play together as lovers do and he would feel her breasts, and put his hands through the slits of her gown and up her petticoats; and my mistress in return would tickle the defendant, beat pull and strike him amorously etc."

The jury retired for twenty minutes and agreed on a fine of one thousand pounds. The admiral had been demanding ten times that sum.

53. The Master Stroke.

The clergy were not spared the trauma of having their sexual exploits dragged through the courts. The Reverend John Craven was once again exposed by a chambermaid who stated that he:

> "had his hands up Mrs. Harris's petticoat and he saw both Mrs. Harris's legs, and one of them as high as the calf."

On seeing her mistress go into the bedroom the servant went and listened some minutes at the door, during which time she heard the bed crack but did not hear a word spoken. There were several marks or spots upon the sheets, which they believed were caused by Mr. Craven and Mrs. Harris lying together the previous night.

Sentence of divorce from 'bed board and mutual cohabitation' was passed in the usual way against Mrs. Harris.

The language used in the court reports of the eighteenth century is as interesting as many of the divorce cases themselves. The case against Mr. John Arnold, a watchmaker charged with cruelty to his wife and for committing adultery with Margaret Wood, is typical of the day and may not have been re-told for over two hundred years.

54. The shame of an appearance in the Divorce Court.

HE WAS HER MAN, BUT HE DONE HER WRONG

Mrs. Arnold, in her libel dated December 10, 1767, against her husband, stated that she was of an affable temper and modest carriage, of a religious and virtuous life and conversation, and always behaved to Mr. Arnold with great duty and respect and as a dutiful wife; that her husband was of a surly, morose, cruel, passionate, and violent temper, and of a lewd and vicious disposition; that he had foresaken her company, and entered into adulterous conversation with diverse lewd women; that he had often cruelly beaten her, uttering at the same time indecent language and dreadful threats; that, instigated by the devil and his own carnal lust and inelination, in April, 1766, he entered into a lewd, scandalous and adulterous, acquaintance with one Margaret Wood; that in November, 1766, he took lodgings at Mr. Peter Horsey's in Coldbath fields where he and Mrs. Wood went by the fictitious name of Jackson, and pretended to be man and wife; that they continued there as man and wife till April, 1767, lying in one bed together, naked and alone, and there committing the said crime of adultery; that he withdrew himself from her bed, would not allow her to eat at table with him or come into his presence, but kept her confined in a back room, and would not permit any victuals to be carried to her till all the rest of the family had dined; that on the 29th November, 1767, in the evening, she went into his bedchamber, where he was in bed, and enquired of him with great humility how she had been so unhappy as to have lost his affection, and what she could do to regain it; on which he started from his bed, knocked her down to the ground with his doubled fists, and there beat, kicked and cruelly treated her, till the people in the house came to her rescue; that when confined in the back room, the servants were ordered not to mind what she said; that he had endeavoured to prevail on different persons to commence an intrigue with her, often saying he would give a hundred pounds to any man that would debauch her, or fifty pounds for news of her death; that on account of the blows, wounds, bruises, kicks and other ill-treatment of her husband, she was reduced to a very ill state of health, and her cohabitation with him had become dangerous on account of his cruelty; that he had not rendered her conjugal rites since October, 1766; that he did not allow her any maintenance, and to prevent her from receiving any relief or credit whatsoever since the commencement of this suit, caused the following advertisement to be printed in the Daily Advertiser on the 28th, 29th and 30th of September, 1767.

> "Whereas Dorothy Arnold, the wife of John Arnold, hath agreed to live separate and apart from me, and I do allow her a separate maintenance, this is to caution all persons not to give her any credit as I will not pay any debts she may contract.
>
> *John Arnold*
> *Sept. 23, 1767.   Watch-maker, Devereaux court."*

Therefore Mrs. Arnold prayed that she might be divorced from bed, board, and mutual cohabitation with her husband.

It was also set forth that he made annually six hundred pounds.

55. Wives discover husbands about to give in to temptation.

Mrs. Sarah Horsey of Coldbath fields, deposed that, under the name of Jackson, Mr. Arnold and Margaret Wood hired a lodging in her second floor in November, 1766, saying they were newly married; they lived there six months as man and wife, lying together in the same bed; that in May, 1767, they went to live in Mr. Arnold's house, Devereaux-court.

Other evidences, their own servants and neighbours in Devereaux-court, deposed that Mrs. Arnold was a sober virtuous woman and her husband a wicked debauched man; that Margaret Wood lay in the same bed with Mr. Arnold; Elizabeth Hawkes in particular, a maid-servant, that she made but one bed for them, and had observed that two persons had lain in it, particularly that a man and a woman had lain therein; and she believed that at such times Mr. Arnold had carnal use and knowledge of the body of the said Margaret Wood; that at one time there was cause to believe that Margaret Wood had miscarried.

Mr. L'Argeau deposed that Mr. Arnold and his wife had a daughter; that in December, 1766, Mrs. Arnold appeared to be very much hurt — her head swelled, and a cut through her upper lip — which she said had been done by her husband.

Mary Raitt, servant, deposed that Mr. Arnold often called his wife by the most opprobrious names; that she had heard him beat her twice, and Mrs. Arnold called out murder, and a little time after that she found her in a bloody condition, with her face much bruised. Another time he had beaten her so much about the mouth, and it swelled so much that she could not eat for a day or two but with a small tea-spoon; another time he threw a quantity of beer over her, and she appeared to have received such a violent blow on the arm, that the evidence thought it in danger of mortifying, and she was deprived of the use of it for some time.

Several witnesses confirmed all the circumstances of ill-usage narrated above, and also the carnal conversation and adultery with Margaret Wood: it would be mere repetition to give them over again.

In regard to Mr. Arnold's yearly income, Mr. Matthews of Fleet Street, watchmaker, deposed that Mr. Arnold carried on a considerable trade, and had the best prices given him, and that he believed his profits annually mounted to three hundred pounds; and Mr. Hyham, watchmaker, of Clements' Lane, Lombard Street, deposed that Mr. Arnold had often told him, within the last two or three years, that he got three hundred pounds a year.

Sentence of divorce and separation was given in the usual form and Mr. Arnold was adjudged to pay his wife twenty pounds yearly in equal quarterly payments.

THE EVIL THAT MEN DO...

The case of the alleged rape of Anne Bond in 1729 highlighted the vulnerability of young girls to the prey of truly evil men:

'Anne Bond deposed, that, being out of place and having been ill, she happened to be sitting on a bench at her lodging, and a woman whom she knew not, took an occasion to enter into conversation with her, and asked her if she wanted a place, telling her she was very serviceable in helping servants to places; she replying she would willingly embrace a good service, she told her she could help her to a very good one, which was to one Colonel Harvey; accordingly she went, was hired, and did not know for three days but that the prisoner's name was Harvey.

(The prisoner in the dock was Colonel Francis Charteris, who used the pseudonym Harvey, he had pleaded not guilty to the charge of attempting to ravish Anne Bond.)

For the first three days she was treated well; he sent his footman with her and he redeemed some clothes she had been obliged to pawn. After three days he began to solicit her to let him lie with her offering her a great purse of gold, telling her he would give her a great many fine clothes, get her a good husband, would give her a house, he having a great many, if she would go to bed with him; she told him she would take none of his money on any such account.

(Anne Bond discovered that her employer's real name was Charteris and tried to leave the household as she knew of his reputation.)

She added, when I offered to go away, he threatened my life, and I was kept in, and not permitted to go out of the house, the doors being kept locked, and if the clerk of the kitchen went out, the housekeeper or butler had the key, so that I could never get out after the three or four days. She went to live with the prisoner about the 24th of October and came away the 10th of November.

On the 10th of November, the colonel rung a bell, and bid the clerk of the kitchen call the Lancashire b_____h into the dining room. On going in he bid her stir the fire; while she was doing it he locked the door and took her and threw her down on the couch, which was nigh the fire, in the farther corner of the room, and forced her down with violence and lay with her; she strove what she could and cried out as loud as she could, and he took off his night-cap and thrust it into her mouth and then had carnal knowledge of her against her will.'

The Colonel spent some time in Newgate for the offence but probably as a result of his wealth he was out within a reasonably short space of time as his death was recorded two years later.

'Francis Charteris was a man infamous for all manner of vices. When he was an ensign in the army he was drummed out of the regiment for a cheat; he was next banished to Brussels and drummed out of Ghent on the same account. After a hundred tricks at the gaming-tables, he took to lending of money at exorbitant interest, and capital, into a new capital, and seizing to a minute when the payments became due. In a word, by a constant attention to the vices, wants and follies of mankind he acquired an immense fortune. His house was a perpetual bawdy-house. He was twice condemned for rapes and pardoned, but the last time not without imprisonment in Newgate, and large confiscations. He died in Scotland in 1731, aged 62. The populace at his funeral raised a great riot, almost tore the body out of the coffin, and cast dead dogs and cats into the grave along with it.'

56. The ill-timed interruption.

THE ACTRESS AND THE ARISTOCRAT

If the advice of not putting one's daughters on the stage had been offered to Mrs. Bilton in the 1880's, instead of Missis. Worthington some time later, then Belle and Flo would almost certainly have settled for lives of dull domesticity in the grubby garrison suburb of Woolwich in South-East London. Being home to the Royal Artillery they would probably have married soldiers and had to endure the overcrowded harsh living conditions and almost perpetual pregnancy of their peers.

That they went on to lead a very different and much more eventful life might be put down to three reasons: looks, laughter and luck. As any budding entertainer knows, by far the most important of the three is luck if they are ever to rise from obscurity. The Bilton girls had the good fortune to be spotted in their very first stage production. Flo,14, and Belle, 13, were pushed into service as extras in an amateur pantomime at Woolwich garrison in 1881. As chance would have it a theatrical agent spotted potential in the two girls and made them an offer that would change their lives forever.

After asking and receiving permission from their parents, the agent took the girls on the road as a song and dance routine. With the vitality of youth, the happy, healthy girls immediately dispelled all their audience's memories of ten hour shifts of backbreaking work. They quickly rose to the top of the bill commanding a weekly wage of some £30 a week, some thirty times more than they may have expected in a factory job in Woolwich. The girls enchanted the audiences with their songs openly expressing their joie-de-vivre. The whole audience would lustily join the refrains and all problems were forgotten for an hour or two as they sang in harmony.

Belle, the younger of the girls, was the most sought after and swiftly became one of the first highly popular pin-ups. One of her many admirers described her as a 19-year-old: [She has] 'a curious individual charm, and a haunting look of tragedy in her expression that made an irresistible appeal.'

The tragedy was still to be played out.

Belle became infatuated with a smooth talking conman, Alden Carter Weston. He whispered the sweet nothings that all young girls like to hear and believe. He forgot, however, to mention that he was married and that his income was derived by conning vulnerable people out of their savings. Belle fell pregnant as Weston was sentenced to eighteen months. It seemed that a rags to riches story was in serious danger of going into reverse.

The vivacious Belle, however, had no shortage of admirers amongst the rich young beaus. Isidor Emmanuel Wertheimer introduced himself to the young damsel in distress. Without asking for a penny piece, he funded the services of a doctor and nurse until her baby was born. Belle then moved into her benefactor's house in St. John's Wood. Isidor later admitted that he had asked for the young mother's hand in marriage but Belle remained faithful to the baby's father. Both parties denied that there was any sexual relationship between them, denials which they were later forced to repeat in court.

To the well-to-do, actresses were little more than trollops and gold-diggers. When Isidor told his father that he wished to marry Belle, he was immediately given a one-way berth to America so that his passion might wane with the distance and passing of time. It appears that parents had a little more control of their offspring than is the case today.

Belle was on her own again...but not for long.

William Frederick Le Poer Trench, better known as Viscount Dunlo, despite heavy expenditure on his schooling, was never destined to be one of the countries academics. To put it more bluntly he was as thick as three planks as far as examinations were concerned and failed the relatively simple test for admission to Sandhurst. His excuse for not qualifying to become one of the asses that led the lions in WW1 was that he was more than a little partial to what he considered the good things in life: partying, procreation and punting, and who would blame him?

Dunlo chose fast women and slow horses and within a week of meeting Belle was besotted. The heir to over 25,000 acres in Galway and Roscommon rashly proposed marriage and one month later, on July 10th 1889, the couple, both 21, tied the knot in Hampstead Registrar's office. Dunlo's father was not present for the simple reason that he knew nothing about the ceremony or even the existence of Belle Bilton.

The Viscount was a weak man. He told both his parents and his wife what they wanted to hear even though, if compared, the letters would be contradictory. The day after his wedding he wrote to his father:

56a. Florence Bilton - the second half of the double act in the rags to riches story.

56b. Belle Bilton, later Lady Dunlo and the fifth Countess of Clancarty.

> "...I believe I really am married, and there is no use denying it. Why I did it I don't know. I have no excuse to make. I can't say I was drunk. I don't think I was. Still I believe I must have been off my head during the last few months...
>
> I think that the sooner I go away the better. I should like to remain abroad as long as possible."

A few days later a second father was packing off a son to the far corners of the globe for taking up with the 'common' Belle Bilton. Lord Clancarty, Dunlo's father, refused to acknowledge the existence of the young actress. He took no half-measures, procuring passage for his son on a ship bound for Australia.

During his son's 'voluntary' exile, Lord Clancarty set about having the marriage dissolved and employed private detectives to uncover any dirt they could find about his unwanted daughter-in-law.

As one admirer left, another returned to Belle. Wertheimer, her first 'platonic' benefactor had sailed back from America and, despite his father's protestations, persuaded her to set up home with him.

Meanwhile absence was certainly making the heart grow fonder. As his father's employees were sniffing out grounds for divorce, the weak-willed Dunlo was writing from Sydney to the woman he had loved and left, his wife:

> "Belle, I do nothing but think of you all day, and dream of you all night. I love you truly. I never think of anyone but you, my pretty Belle."

In a separate letter to his father he agreed to divorce Belle!

Dunlo did not find life in the colonies to his taste and returned in the summer of 1890. It appears that his fear of his father was greater than his love for his wife. He was persuaded to proceed with an action to divorce Belle claiming that she had been having an affair with the man whose home she shared. Dunlo v Dunlo and Wertheimer, the actress and aristocrat revealing their dirty washing in public, was the kind of juicy entertainment so beloved of all levels of society. On the opening day the court was packed to overflowing and police reinforcements were drafted in to clear the gangways.

All eyes were on the beautiful Lady Dunlo (formerly Belle Bilton) and her sister who were used to public performances. Belle, throughout the case, vigorously denied the charges of adultery.

A number of unconvincing witnesses were called but none would swear on oath that they had seen Lady Dunlo and Wertheimer in bed together. A waiter from a hotel in Trouville crossed the Channel to testify that the couple had stayed in his hotel, but, following questions from the defence, he acknowledged that they had separate rooms.

Two private detectives, who had disguised themselves when spying on the couple, admitted that on occasions they had peeked through the keyholes in rooms where Belle had been staying but found no evidence of adultery. Indeed the longer the case went on the more farcical it became. A coachman was asked whether Wertheimer had put his arm around Lady Dunlo in his cab. Much to the amusement of the spectators in the packed court he replied:

> "Yes I did, guv'nor, and I'd have done it myself if I'd had half a chance."

Another witness added that during a pantomime in Manchester he had seen Lady Dunlo 'smoking a cigarette and drinking champagne with Isidor Wertheimer'. When questioned as to why he was giving evidence the witness replied that Lady Dunlo had not paid his commission for finding her an engagement in Manchester! Rather than the laughter in court that followed the case should have been laughed out of court. The jury took just fifteen minutes to find for Lady Dunlo.

Following the newspaper coverage of the case, Belle swiftly became one of the most famous women in the country. Agents and theatre managers were falling over each other in their efforts to sign her up, some offering over £100 per night to appear in music-hall. She was billed as 'Miss Belle Bilton (Lady Dunlo)' and there was never a spare seat in the house.

With the death some months later of her father-in-law, the Earl of Clancarty, who had been the main protagonist in the court case, Belle's husband, who had never really wanted a divorce, inherited the title. The couple re-united and went to spend the rest of their days in Ireland. They produced five children, but unlike the fairy story it in some ways resembles, the couple did not live happily ever after. The young chorus girl plucked from obscurity in Woolwich and eventually given the title of Lady died after a long and brave fight against cancer. She was 37 years old.

57. Campbell versus Campbell. Lord Colin accused of adultery with the Maid, Lady Campbell with the Chief of the London Fire Brigade, her Doctor and a Captain. Neither case was proved.

'LOVE IS LIKE LINEN — OFTEN CHANGED, THE SWEETER'

Not just one but at least twelve people looked through the keyhole in the notorious Campbell versus Campbell proceedings in 1888. The whole jury were invited to the residence of Lord Colin and Lady Colin Campbell to witness what might have been observed through the keyhole. They were to leave disappointed as very little could be seen and the case of the Lord's alleged adultery with a servant girl had to be dropped. Lady Campbell had accused her husband of infecting her with syphilis on their honeymoon, being bi-sexual and having had intercourse with Mary Wilson, the former housemaid. After a medical examination she was declared a virgin.

Mary did however seem to implicate her mistress as they had a secret code between them which alerted Lady Colin to the fact that one of her alleged lovers had arrived. The code was: 'Please, my lady, cook wants to see you.'

This alleged lover was to become the future Duke of Marlborough. Lady Colin Campbell's husband also accused her of adultery with a Captain, the chief of the London Fire Brigade and her Doctor. Lady Colin was a voluptuous woman who enjoyed life to the full, displaying her charms to Whistler who nicknamed her 'lovely leopard' after painting her in the nude. The good Lady's defence was that she had no time for adultery and after a court case lasting nearly three weeks and costing a great deal of money, the jury could not confirm adultery by either party.

CHARLES DILKE; 'LYING IN STATE'

Three people sharing the same bed was accepted as an economic necessity in the slums of the East End but when it became a regular occurrence between the sheets of a Cabinet Minister the press and public began to show more than a little interest.

Charles Dilke was tipped to succeed Gladstone as Prime Minister before his world fell apart at the age of forty-three. He was forced to appear at the divorce of Donald Crawford and his twenty-three-year-old wife Virginia who testified that he had taken her to an 'afternoon house' and later made love to her. The jury was outraged by her further accusations. Virginia stated that Dilke had said that he wanted to see both her and the maid, Fanny, together. When Charles and Virginia were in bed Charles said he wanted Fanny who duly appeared in the altogether and joined the couple. With Virginia on one side and Fanny on the other Charles was probably in a quandary as to which way to turn. Virginia alleged that these sessions took place over a period of two-and-a-half years during which time Dilke taught Virginia 'every French vice.' Whether Fanny picked anything up we shall never know as she did not give evidence at the trial but denied the accusations outside the court.

Whether Dilke engaged in troilism or not he was found guilty by the press and was prevented from reaching his full potential. It was later proved that Virginia was as much at home with three in a bed as two as she went hunting with her sister for men who would like to make up a threesome. Later in life Virginia turned to the Catholic Church and devoted all her time and energy to social work and writing religious and social books.

BEFORE THE MAST

Not all cases went to court, many taking the law into their own hands. Archenoltz relates two such tales:

> 'A ship's captain came upon his wife and one of his sailors when they expected not to be disturbed in what they were doing. He had her stripped naked and, with her lover, set astride a mast which was decked with streamers and carried on the shoulders of a number of sailors. The procession went through the streets of East London while a band played and an amazing crowd of people followed.'

> 'A country nobleman, who had come with his wife to London on a pleasure trip, had strong suspicions of her infidelity. He gave out he was going on a journey and surprised her in the night in the arms of an officer. He was provided with cord and had them bound by men hand and foot and tied by the neck to the bed-posts. He exhibited them in this plight to all his friends and acquaintances. The friends brought others along, for which permission was gladly given and this strange spectacle lasted for four days, during which time the loving couple got nothing but bread and water.'

DILKE : "Hullo ! Maskelyne and Cook are performing one of my tricks !"

How many disappearing ladies are there about ? Since Fanny vanished so mysteriously there seem to be no end to the young ladies who depart and leave no traces of the method of their flitting. Buatier de Kolta claims to be the inventor of this trick and not Sir Charles Dilke, as many have been led to believe. De Kolta's method, as exemplified by Mr. Charles Bertram, may be witnessed daily at Messrs. Maskelyne and Cook's. It is quite as good a performance as the one brought before the public and Sir James Hannen a little while ago.

58. Charles Dilke. Accusations of troilism ruined his career.

STRANGE STORIES OF THE CAPITAL'S ECCENTRICS

59. Standing on the corner watching all the girls go by.

England has long been known worldwide for the high number of eccentrics, many of whom were drawn to London.

After a lifetime of gambling and debauchery it might be suspected that William Douglas would spend what years remained after his eightieth birthday gardening or reminiscing with cronies. He had other ideas and every day could be found in his house in Piccadilly admiring all the young women who passed on the pavement below. He kept his groom permanently standing by the door and if any young girl — from whatever background — took his fancy she was enticed in and invited to join the Duke or 'Old Q' as he was to become famous as, in the old man's insane eccentricities where he put into practice all his sexual fantasies. Being a man of considerable means, very few rejected the invitation.

One of Old Q's acquaintances described his last few years:

> 'He sought for pleasure in all its forms, and was as eager for it at 80 as he had been when only 20. Having exhausted all the imaginable pleasures of human life, he settled down in his house near Hyde Park corner, looking out of his windows at what Johnson had called "the full stream of human life."
> ... It is however a fact that he performed the scene of Paris and the three goddesses in his dressing room; three of the most wonderfully beautiful girls in London were brought there, dressed like the Homeric goddesses on the Mount of Ida, whilst he, in a shepherd's costume rewarded the one he considered the most beautiful with a golden apple.'

It was rumoured that Old Q bathed in milk, but this was denied by those who knew him well though he did live a rather eccentric old age. At seven in the morning he took his breakfast of coffee and buttered muffin in the bath. He ate regularly throughout the day and at midnight consumed a supper of roast pullet with lime punch. At three o'clock every morning he was awakened by his servant to devour a savoury veal cutlet washed down with wine and water. He slept again to his next bath a few hours later.

When he died in 1810 his bed was covered with over seventy love letters which he had been unable to open. They emanated from women in every walk of life.

JUST HANGING AROUND

Kotzwarra was a brilliant musician being able to play thirteen instruments; one of the most renowned big bass players in Europe he had many admirers including Bach. He was also a sexual deviant. Forever seeking greater satisfaction than normal intercourse could provide he chose to follow an extremely dangerous path. Having been told that a hanged person experienced for several minutes a very pleasant sensation due to the accelerated circulation of the blood and the distention of certain vessels, Kotzwarra had hanged himself in several prostitutes' rooms telling them to cut him down after five minutes.

Susanna Hill was not too keen on the idea but was eventually persuaded. Unfortunately for the musician the prostitute's timekeeping was not all it might have been and he never recovered consciousness.

In the early 1770s Susanna Hill was put on trial for murder. All women were ordered to leave the court and all printed matter relating to the case ordered to be burnt. Evidence from Susanna was however printed and the story is best told in one of the leaked documents.

> "On the afternoon of the 2nd September, between the hours of one and two O'clock, a man whom she had never seen before and who was identical with the deceased, came to the house where she is staying, the street door having been open. He asked her whether she would like to have a drink with him. She wanted porter, he brandy and water, and he gave her money to fetch the drinks, as well as some mutton and beef, which she also purchased. After a time they retired together to a back room where several most indecent acts took place. Then he said he would like to be hanged for five minutes and, while giving her some money to buy a rope, he observed that this would increase his pleasure and produce the desired effect. She then fetched two thin ropes which she placed round his neck. He pulled himself up on the door of the back room, pulling up his legs, so that he hung very low. After five minutes she cut him off and he immediately fell to the floor. She thought that he had become unconscious and called a woman living opposite to her assistance . . ."

The accused was acquitted.

A GOOD SPANKING NEVER DID ANYONE ANY HARM

Is it by chance that more has been written about English sexual behaviour by German historians than by British? They tend to overemphasise the practice of flagellation, creating the impression that the English like nothing more than giving or receiving a good spanking! Some examples of the occurrence of these dubious pleasures are recorded below though it must be remembered that this behaviour was the exception rather than the rule.

In the Bon Ton Magazine of December 1792 there appears a detailed account of the proceedings at a female flagellation club which met every Thursday evening in Jermyn Street:

> "These feminine members were mostly married women, who, being tired of marriage in its normal form and of the cold indifference which after a time supervenes in the conjugal relationship, decided to employ other means to bring back the ecstasy which they experienced at the beginning of their marriage.

> "The worthy company or 'club' of which we speak, never has less than twelve members, six of whom are in each case chastised by the other six. They draw lots as to which group should come first, after which a lecture or an extempore speech is given, describing the effects of flagellation as practised from the earliest times to the present day at monasteries, convents, brothels and private houses. Then the six passive women take up their positions and their active partners strip such parts of their bodies as are not only less visible and less easily accessible for chastisement than others, but also — and all the more — sensitive; and the practical work now commences. The chairwoman of the club hands each of the active group a big rod and starts to flagellate, with any variation she chooses, while the others look on.

> Sometimes, in accordance with the chairwoman's directions, flagellation begins on the calves and gradually rises to the buttocks, until the whole region which was at first 'white as milk', becomes suffused with red."

60. The famous Berkley Horse, made its inventor Theresa, a rich and popular woman.

Vast fortunes have been made by supplying an unfilled demand. Finding a hole in the market is every entrepreneur's dream and this was realised by Theresa Berkley in the early 1800s when she set up shop in Portland Place. The market she served was for those who enjoyed a spanking and she was more than well equipped to serve every taste.

'Her supply of birch was extensive, and kept in water, so that it was always green and pliant; she had shafts with a dozen whip thongs on each of them; a dozen different sizes of cat-o'nine tails, some with needle points worked into them; various kinds of thin bending canes; leather straps like coach traces; battledoors, made of thick sole-leather, with inch nails run through to docket, and currycomb tough hides rendered callous by many years flagellation. Holly brushes, furze brushes; a prickly evergreen, called butcher's bush; and during the summer, glass and China vases, filled with a constant supply of green nettles, with which she often restored the dead to life.

Thus, at her stop, whoever went with plenty of money, could be birched, whipped, fustigated, scourged, needle-pricked, half-hung, holly-brushed, furze-brushed, stinging-nettled, curry-combed, phlebotomized and tortured till he had a belly full.''

SARAH POTTER

In the 1860's Sarah Potter was sentenced to six months hard labour for allowing girls to be beaten in brothels run by her in Wardour Street and Kings Road, Chelsea. The following accounts were published by The Times in 1863.

'Catherine Kennedy, about 17 years of age, was next examined. She entered the prisoner's house in Wardour Street about January last. For about three days she was asked by the prisoner to allow herself to be flogged with birch rods by gentlemen. She was in want of money and submitted. She was strapped to a folding ladder, without any clothes on. After she was flogged the gentlemen gave her a sovereign. The room in which she was flogged was called the 'schoolroom'. She was flogged on a second occasion for about ten minutes very severely. She received half a sovereign for that flogging, and left the next day.

Alice Smith said that in February she was first introduced to the prisoner in Wardour Street. She had not long been there before she was told by the prisoner to go into the schoolroom. She found there a short, fat gentleman. He was standing by a ladder, and there were rods lying on a sofa. She was fastened to a ladder with straps and then flogged. The prisoner was in the room standing by the door. The lashes were very severe, and she screamed. She asked them to let her go, and called out 'Police!' and said that she could bear it no longer. The flogging brought blood from her person. She had no power to release herself, as she was tied to the ladder. She got no money on that occasion.'

Several papers, whilst apparently disapproving of the letters contained in their columns, knew that such material helped their sales enormously. Spanking news from around the world was of great interest to the people in Victorian days and newspapers have changed little in over one hundred years. After reading the sport, on Sunday the reader might settle back with a copy of Town Talk or Society and be pleasantly outraged by the following letters:

'I think many women will agree with me that there is pleasure in being tightly laced by one's husband. Once my husband asked me to whip him, which I did severely, having first laced him in a pair of my stays. We have been great friends since, but one of us is sure to get a whipping before long.'
WASP-WAIST (Society, 1899)

SIR — May I ask whether you or any of your readers have ever heard of a vile practice of birching of men and women who have been paid for their services? I am led to believe that this is now in vogue. If it is, it is a form of vice which should be speedily stamped out. — yours, etc. TRUTH (Town Talk, 1884)

George IV was a great believer in the power of truffles to act as a sexual stimulant and he asked that all Italian Ambassadors should send them by special courier to London to bolster his flagging sexual appetite.

Travels abroad often influenced a Londoner's way of life. After a stay in India a man rented a house near Soho Square. His wife took charge of his private harem of six girls, they all sleeping in the same room, their beds arranged in a circle so the 'master' could do his evening round!

Lord Baltimore lived out his fantasies in a super house he had built in the West End. The decor was based on a celebrated harem in Constantinople. He employed a number of attractive women to satisfy his every whim and when he tired of them discharged them with magnificent presents and sometimes a handsome dowry.

One of Lord Milton's sons decided to go out with a bang. He presented himself at one of the most fashionable brothels and asked for twelve of the most attractive girls to be sent to his room. He entertained the young ladies to his last supper, a sumptuous one, and then closed the doors, never to see daylight again.

He ordered the girls to undress and entertain him as best they knew how with voluptuous poses and dances for several hours. He duly rewarded the girls for their entertainment and shot himself. With a smile on his face?

One English nobleman tired of being a bachelor. After a sleepless night he sent for his valet and announced that he would marry the first woman he met that morning. The valet returns below stairs and informs the housekeeper that she is wanted by the master of the house. The nobleman comes straight to the point and asks the employee to dress herself for church immediately as they are to be married that morning. In his turn the soon-to-be-married gentleman prepares himself and half an hour later rings once again for his valet. Upon demanding news as to the whereabouts of his bride to be, he is informed that she is busy with the housework, thinking her master to be 'in jest!' The vexed nobleman orders a 'kitchen wench' to be sent up and the couple are married within the hour.

An unusual sale took place in 1840 when the collection of an anatomical lecturer was put up for sale, the items including the penis of Captain Nicholls who had died in Horsemonger Lane Jail five years previously. A second penis, that of a private in the blues, had been bottled in a glass twelve inches long and the auctioneer guaranteed it to be in a perfect state of preservation. The private part fetched a healthy price.

When Lord Southesk discovered that his wife was having an affair with the Duke of York, he conceived a most original revenge:

> 'He went to the most infamous places, to seek for the most infamous disease (V.D.) which he met with; but his revenge was only half completed; for after he had gone through every remedy to get quit of his disease, his lady did but return him his present, having no more connection with the person for whom it was so industriously prepared.'

In the 1700's a guardsman and three women were accused of 'being found in bed all together. 'All three women were sent to prison but the soldier argued 'that he had undergone enough punishment fornicating with three women at the same time.' He was allowed to go about his business.

Harriet had a pretty bosom and effeminate qualities, or so she tells us in her memoirs. She could also swear like a sailor but was nobody's fool. When she fell in love with Lord Ponsonby she knew he would soon tire of her if she could not hold a decent conversation. Locking herself away in her room, and only appearing for ten minutes at a time to bolt down a meal, Harriet took to reading, the Greeks for two whole days, the Romans six more, then Rousseau's confessions, Racine's tragedies and Boswell's 'Life of Johnson.'

"For fear of dying in the night and not making an elegant corpse" Harriet paid as much attention to her nightwear as she did her day clothes. She described her first meeting with her beloved Lord:

> "I heard the knock, and his footsteps on the stairs; and then that most godlike head uncovered, that countenance so pale, so still, so expressive, the mouth of such perfect loveliness, the fine, clear, transparent, dark skin . . ."

Harriet burst into tears, but the couple did not kiss on the first night:

> "No, not tonight, I could not bear your kiss tonight. We will dream about it until tomorrow."

The Lord treated Harriet with great delicacy.

She would sometimes wait for hours on end in a Hackney coach outside the House of Lords 'merely for one more kiss and the pleasure of driving with him to his own door.' For his part Lord Ponsonby would carry one of Harriet's shoes in his pocket 'as a pattern to guide him in his constant search after pretty shoes for her'.

With the coming of the railways and the growing independence of women some men lived in fear of meeting a female in an empty carriage. Sir William Hardman noted in his diary:

> "I was put in a beastly funk the other day by a woman. I had travelled towards town as far as Wandsworth in a compartment to myself when a female got in; she had her hair in short curls and wore no gloves. She first of all sat in the opposite seat, then she moved to the opposite corner, then to the middle, three seats in as many minutes! I began to speculate as to where she would sit next — perhaps on my knee, and then would charge me with an indecent assault. Happily she got out at the next station, Clapham Junction, but my mind was not at ease, for she stood outside the carriage door and just as the train started, got into the next compartment. I assure you I was much exercised by this little adventure."

61. Sir William Hardman's worst nightmare.

62. Risqué photographs were imported from Paris.

63. Early evening.

LOVE AND PRIDE STOCK BEDLAM

Agnes disappeared whilst walking with her father along the Strand. The noted Victorian astronomer, James Ferguson, must have had his head in the clouds. One minute he was holding his teenage daughter's hand, the next she had disappeared from his sight forever. A frantic search was made and advertisements published throughout London, all to no avail. Agnes had seemingly vanished from the face of the earth.

It was the young girl's infatuation with one of her father's students that led to her disappearance. Picking a time when her absence would not be noticed Agnes stole off — down one of the many sidestreets and into the arms of her nobleman lover, the couple immediately fleeing to Italy.

The elopement did not lead to the happy ending that both parties desired and Agnes's paramour deserted her, leaving the poor girl broken-hearted and destitute... Being too ashamed to return to her "Victorian" parents she tried to earn a living as best she could. Garrick, the famous theatre impressario assisted her journey back to England and gave her a trial as an actress. Having no aptitude for this role and with her attempts at writing even less successful, she was forced to join the thousands of ladies "on the streets". The miserable poverty led to her premature death some years later, just a few yards from where she had made that fateful decision as a starry-eyed girl all those years before.

Agnes told her story to the doctor just before she passed away and related how she had often seen her rich relations pass her on the streets, but was too ashamed to present herself.

Many rich women of the aristocracy used to seek excitement in shoplifting though many of them could have afforded to buy the total contents of the shop. One woman used to replace all the goods she had stolen the following day. One young and attractive girl was caught red-handed by a shop-assistant. He threatened to denounce her as a thief unless she took him as her husband. The couple were married and the shop assistant received a present of some £12,000.

Sometimes odd little things annoy us but we are helpless to remedy them. For some reason the sight of footmen adorning the backs of carriages used to annoy the author John Heneage Jesse, who took a dislike particularly to their powdered heads and impeccable appearance. With his stick at the ready he would position himself in St. James's Street so that he could dip it into the mud and puddles and deliberately soil the immaculate attire of the passing coachman commonly known as 'catch farts' who dare not relax their hold lest they fall from their carriages.

On a visit to London Zoo Charles Waterton entered the cage of a large orangoutan and took it upon himself to give the animal a dental examination. The orangoutan then swapped positions and proceeded to examine Mr. Waterton's teeth and mouth. At other times in the middle of a conversation, in mid-sentence, he would make for the nearest tree and shin to the top.

If you called on Jack Black in Battersea, the chances are he would open the door with an old rat squatting on his shoulder and others crawling about inside his clothes. He was the self-appointed 'Rat and Mole Destroyer to Her Majesty'. The elderly man had V.R. embroidered on his coat and showed a great deal of expertise in catching and handling rodents.

He was equally at home with birds and would cage and train song birds. Blackbirds, finches, starlings and nightingales were imprisoned in tiny cages and sold in the London Markets around Bethnal Green. The birds would be taught to sing by darkening the cage and playing a simple air on a pipe, or even by whistling, until the bird would imitate it perfectly.

We all know people who are rather slow to buy a round of drinks and reluctant to put their hand in their pockets. Few, however, can be as tight as certain eighteenth century misers. Sir James Lowther had an annual income of some £40,000 but after paying 2d for a dish of coffee returned to the coffee-house, complaining that he had been given a bad ½d in his change and demanded a replacement. Sir Robert Brown used to tot up how much he saved by never having an orange or lemon on his sideboard. His total material wealth consisted of a large wig — given to him of course — though he had made a fortune as a merchant in Venice. All three of his daughters died of consumption and when told that horse-riding might improve their health Sir Robert drew up a map of London and a route which would not pass through any turnpikes so he would not have to pay the toll. The undertaker was summoned to meet the three girls before they died and they promised to be his friend so they might secure a cheaper burial.

The M.P. Mr. Elwes, to save going to the butcher, had a whole sheep killed and ate only mutton until it was exhausted... He would not allow his shoes to be cleaned lest they wear out more quickly and denied himself any fire by daylight or sheets at night but would get up and keep himself warm by counting his money. He left property to the value of £800,000.

The death of a loved one affects us all in different ways. Dr. Van Buchell could not bear to be parted from his recently deceased first wife and employed a Dr. Hunter, in 1775, to preserve her body. This he did by injecting the blood-vessels with carmine fluid. Glass eyes were then inserted and all the cavities packed. The corpse was subsequently dressed in silk and lace and laid upon a bed, hidden by a curtain. The body was kept in the living room and guests introduced to the 'dear departed' for several years. The practice was only put to an end after the doctor's second marriage.

Almost opposite Liverpool Street Station stands one of London's most famous pubs. After the death of his father in 1761 Nathaniel Bentley inherited a great deal of money from the prosperous hardware business. As any young man would do today he decided to spend, spend, spend. His appearance was immaculate as he always dressed in the height of fashion and became a true dandy. Not surprisingly he was found attractive by the young ladies and he soon fell head-over-heels in love with a beautiful girl.

When his proposal was accepted Nathaniel became the happiest man in the capital and set about making arrangements for a banquet to celebrate the engagement.

In Nathaniel's house the glass and silver were laid out and the best food and wine of the day lay heavily on the oak tables. It was as Nathaniel was preparing a nosegay of flowers for his bride that he received the news that she had died.

Nathaniel immediately ordered the dining room to be locked and not opened again during his lifetime. This command was strictly adhered to even though the young Nathaniel went into a sharp decline. He paid little

64. Fancy dress parties and masked balls might lead to drunken orgies.

attention to himself, rarely washed and became shabby and unkempt. He led the life of a recluse, employing a hired hand to look after his business interests. The only times he was seen was putting up the shutters in the evening and taking them down again in the morning.

Nathaniel died in 1809, but many would argue that his heart was broken forty years earlier. The room could now be opened and the remnants of the feast were discovered. There were also a great number of cobwebs, and the skeletons of rats and mice who had enjoyed the unexpected banquet forty years earlier. The whole room was covered with a thick layer of dust. The story captured the imagination of the locals and it has been speculated that the owners of a pub saw the potential of the story and bought up the contents of the dining room, the pub eventually adopting the name 'Dirty Dick's'.

It is unknown whether Charles Dickens, looking for inspiration, ever visited the pub.

I feel many of us would have met a "Philip Doddrige" at some time in our lives. He was a bachelor who attempted to reform his lady-friends by writing them long letters setting out their faults. He took particular exception to the conversation of one of these 'friends' and wrote to her saying that her vanity had spoilt many a cup of chocolate drunk in his study! He was of course outlining their faults for their own benefit and when he wrote to a widow, Mrs. Jennings, whom he said he found 'pettish and morose' he proposed marriage. It would be to her advantage as if she married him, he could: 'form her more completely, at least to my own fancy.' Her reply contained two letters, although she must surely have been tempted to write just two words.

The 'Mad Marquis' fancied his chances against the hard men of the lower orders. When the Marquis of Waterford came to the capital he would wander through the streets with his friends like a group of football hooligans looking for the local opposition. In an early drink driving offence, the Marquis was arrested after driving along the pavement at 5 a.m. and crashing into a lamp-post. He was fined £2. He would visit gaming clubs and smash up expensive furniture, and would use family portraits for target practice, aiming at the eyes. At an inn he went into a stranger's room with a donkey, trying to introduce the animal into the man's bed and on another occasion he applied aniseed to the hoofs of a clergyman's horse and hunted him down with bloodhounds. He died when crushed beneath his falling horse.

The Duke of Norfolk was not the sort of person to invite out if you were standing a treat. "Jockey" was famous for being able to drink from noon to dawn and suffer no ill-effects. It would not be unusual for him to consume bottles of red wine with one group of friends until they were legless. He would then seek out more drinking companions after eating five rump steaks at one sitting at The Beef Steak Club, this of course being washed down by several bottles of port. He would leave the second group of drinking companions only after they could consume no more and pop in for a fish supper.

Lord Barrymore led both a short and eccentric life. One of his favourite amusements was to drive from the capital to Wargrave in his phaeton. This was an unusually high vehicle for the time and the Duke would whip the windows of the houses he passed with the express intention of cracking them. He proceeded to Vauxhall Gardens to try and cause a riot and then maybe row down to Margate overnight. He once hired a thug off the street and dressed him as a clergyman. The waiters were told to supply him with as much drink as he could handle and Barrymore would take a delight in the mayhem caused by the fighting priest. A shooting accident resulted in Barrymore receiving the full charge from his own gun in his head. He was twenty-four years old.

If certain individuals' behaviour seemed rather eccentric, that of members of clubs was positively insane.

The main aim of the 13 clubs was to challenge fate.

They would meet at a restaurant (after deliberately passing under a ladder), to settle down to thirteen tables, the meals consisting of the same number of courses. Throughout the dinner knives were kept crossed and salt-spoons the shape of gravedigger's spades were employed. And what better way to round off the evening than by smashing several looking-glasses!

65. Two Swells 'slumming it'.

66. Dancing the Cotillion in the 1770's.

The dancing club, consisting mostly of servants, was founded in 1670. The employees would borrow their master's or mistress's clothes and really let themselves go with wild unrestrained dancing. The participants working themselves into a frenzy until they were ready to 'put their arses, by one sort of dancing, in tune for another.'

Ward describes the kind of people who would attend:

> 'To the membership of this club there was no limit to number or quality, but any person was free to shake their rumps and exercise their members to some tune.
>
> The 'bullies, libertines and strumpets' would inevitably seek sexual gratification and those that could not afford to hire one of the retiring rooms would unashamedly perform on the dance floor to the accompaniment of the dancers.'

The beaus club would drink champagne, refresh themselves with snuff and discuss the qualities of court ladies in crude terms:

> 'her heavings, her luscious juicy lips and drowsy leacherous pignies, with all the outward signs that her charming ladyship imparts to signify that she's an indefatigable bedfellow.'

After working themselves up with such talk they would sally forth to attack the women who attended the masked balls.

An outraged writer reported on one of these balls in The Westminster Magazine, May 1774:

> 'A deal of wanton love was exercised to effect purposes most base and dishonourable. The room was crowded with courtezans; there was not a duenna in town who had not brought her Circassians to market; and towards the conclusion of the debauch, I beheld scenes in the rooms upstairs too gross for repetition. I saw ladies and gentlemen together in attitudes and positions that would have disgraced the court of Comus; ladies with their hair dishevelled and their robes almost torn off.'

In Ned Ward's 'History of Clubs' there is to be found a list which probably existed only in the author's imagination, though there were no doubt many eligible for the Ugly Face Club, the Broken Shopkeepers Club and the Lying Club — perhaps Ned himself was president.

Another eccentric group was the Kicking Club; they met at a wine-house or tavern near the court, from whence about midnight they used to sally, dividing themselves into three parties, four persons in each. By the rules of the Society each member was in turn to kick every man he met, and on refusal to forfeit a flask of French claret for the benefit of the club.

After the Restoration the streets of London were in a state of anarchy. There were several 'blasphemous societies' whose favourite pastime was:

> 'for licentious young gentlemen to go about the streets creating an uproar, breaking windows, overturning sedan chairs, thrashing peaceful men, and importuning pretty women with their coarse pleasantries.'

67. *The party in full swing.*

The most famous group were the Mohocks, though many historians feel that their crimes have been exaggerated. They were supposed to have dragged people from the streets and beaten them up and stabbed them. Not content with this they would proceed to stab their victims, cut pieces off them, usually the ears, and roast them.

Anyone they considered below their class was considered 'fair game' and rape was common. In 1712 five 'Peers and Persons of Quality' all Mohocks were involved in a fracas in a tavern in The Strand. The landlady was murdered but this had no effect on the perpetrators of the crime who 'laughed and ordered that she should be added to their bill.' All five were later acquitted.

The Sweaters would surround their victim, their swords drawn and proceed to prick him on 'that part where the schoolboy is punished.'

The Bucks were often fairly well-off and educated but got their 'kicks' by causing mayhem. Their activities would begin at midnight and are here described by one of their own members:

> "We now sallied forth like a pack in full cry, with all the loud expressions of mirth and riot and proceeded to old 77 (a gaming-house) which being shut up, we swore like troopers, and broke the parlour windows in a rage. We next cut the traces of a hackney coach, and led the horses into a mews, where we tied them up; coachee being asleep inside the whole time. We then proceeded to old Ham-a-dry-ed, the bacon's man, called out Fire and got the old man down to the door in his shirt, when Lavender ran away with his night-cap, and threw it into the water in St. James's Square, whilst the Baronet put it in right and left at his sconce, and told him to hide his d_____d ugly masard. This induced him to come out and call the Watch, during which time the buck Parson got into his house, and was very snug with the cook wench until the next evening . . ."

68. "_____ a buck indeed; sings, dances, fights, does everything but read."

CRIME AND PUNISHMENT. EARLY OFFENCES TRIED BY THE CHURCH

An informative guide as to the goings-on both in public and behind locked doors in pre-Victorian times may be discovered by a perusal of church court records relating to the 'correction' of moral offences. These would include all forms of sexual misdemeanours ranging from indecent behaviour towards females to coition with animals. The calling of names; incest, passing on of venereal disease and singing of bawdy songs were also tried by the church and by today's standards fairly lenient sentences were passed.

Non-attendance in church and offences against the Sabbath were deemed as important as the above-mentioned crimes. The battle over Sunday trading still rages today as it did five hundred years ago when innkeepers, blacksmiths and barbers amongst others were charged with working on the Sabbath. A cross-section of the cases, all in London helps show the sort of misdemeanours our ancestors got up to.

In **1476** Master Thomas Ysakyr showed his private parts to many women in the parish.

In **1477** Nicolas Haukyns does not hear divine service but lies in bed in the time of morning service Sunday after Sunday.

In **1481** Joan Gescroft wife of John Gescroft publicly defamed Margaret Baxter in the church of St. Mary at Hyll, calling her a common whore: and she publicly interrupted the calling out of the banns in the said church between the said Margaret and William Lacy, to whom Margaret is betrothed.

In **1482** Thomas Wassyngborn is a heretic; he says that the sacrament of the altar is mere bread; he appears 12 September, denies the charge, and is to appear Monday next.

In **1491** Thomas Nash interrupts church services and causes a commotion by shouting out, on St. Peter's Day and on the feast of the Epiphany, in English. What be you but horis, harlatts and bawdes.

In **1491** Henry Persey haunts taverns shamelessly, and keeps bad company there, suspect women and wicked men.

In **1496** Joan Dyaca is charged that she threw the pax-bread on the ground in church, because another woman kissed it before she did . . . she paid a fine . . . and his lordship ordered her to buy another paxbread and give it to the church.

In **1496** Christopher Kechyn is charged, on the evidence of common fame, that he is a cheat and a seducer of many girls and an adulterer, and he has dishonoured the sacrament of marriage by making a contract of marriage with many women, especially Agnes Moyne, Alice Drystac and Margaret Brok.

In **1518** Agnes Edwards is charged that, according to common fame, she illtreats her husband and does not show him conjugal respect as enjoined by law. Cited, she appears on the 13th of August, and his lordship warns her, under pain of excommunication, to treat her husband better; and he similarly warns Thomas Edwards to treat his wife better.

In **1518** Letticia Wall is to be given a penance. She appears and is sworn and states that she was known by Doctor J.B. and by George Lovekyn, and she cannot be certain which was the father of her child, but she believes in conscience that it was more likely to be George. His lordship orders her to precede the procession next Sunday, with unconcealed face and bare feet and with a wax candle held up in her hand, which candle she is to give to the celebrant at offertory time, and that she is to say the psalm of the Blessed Mary during the mass, and to certify to all this on Monday next in the afternoon.

69. Visit to an early brothel.

In **1632** Mr. Baker the printer. For false printing of the Bible in divers places of it, in the Edition of 1631, vizt. in the 20 of Exodus, 'Thou shalt commit adultery.'

In **1632** Francis Litton. Apprehended in Paules for pissing against a pillar in the Church. The Bishop of London shewed . . . that this man was going through the church to be married, and he could not hould, but must needs ease himself in this inhumane manner. Why did you doe this? Litton fell downe upon his knees and desired mercie, he knew not where he was, he is a countryman and never was at London before, and he knew it not to be a church . . .

EVERY PAGE A PICTURE OF SENSUAL DELIGHTS

Until relatively recently pornography has been written almost exclusively by, and for, men. The tremendous interest in all matters sexual was not satisfied by the stuffy english press and book trade in Victorian times and to satisfy demand a number of what were deemed obscene publications found their way onto the market.

Many were published in France but a number of British printers were tempted to break the law in pursuit of rich returns. Some books were fiction and others purported to give advice on sexual matters. Books would change hands at extremely high prices. A print run might be as low as 125 books with prices starting at a staggering £2 - a month's salary for many workers. In the early days collecting pornographic works was definitely a rich man's pastime. Later in the century songsheets selling the words of bawdy ballads would sell for 6d to satisfy the bottom end of the market.

Details of publications were spread by word of mouth [oral sex?] and buyers would discretely enquire as to what was under the counter in the well-known outlets. Sometimes customers would pay by subscription in advance.

Most of the works were fiction, as were most of those purporting to be fact. Who, however, would not continue reading when presented with the following chapter titles?

> *"Hair on the private parts so luxuriant it was cut off and sold. Copulation prevented by the excessive size of the clitoris. Bestiality with animals, mermen and mermaids, demons and statues. The size of the nose indicative of the yard."*

Moving from 'fact' to fiction, the plot, such as it was in most novels, varied little. Most stories involved a sequence of disjointed chapters of sexual conquests. Nearly every book contained descriptions of the deflowering of young girls, who, at first, resisted sexual advances and then, very quickly, developed a taste for their new sport. All taboo subjects and male fantasies, including back door entry and water sports were catered for in print. The heroes would have sex with their mothers, aunts, sisters, housemaids, prostitutes, nuns and wives of the landed gentry whose husbands could not satisfy them. Many were written in the first person as a kind of secret diary, dating from early experiences with

69a-e. The French photos advertised at the turn of the century seem fairly tame by today's standards.

69b.

69c.

FREE. THE WIVES' & HUSBANDS' HANDBOOK.

Advice to the Wife, Mother, and Husband. 1911 Edition (illustrated), 100 pages. Special information to the Married, with Malthusian advice to both sexes. Special advice free on irregularities and ailments. Various contents. Marriage and its Enjoyments. Health Precautions, Treatment during Confinement. The Baby. Women's Complaints and their Treatment. Common Complaints of Children and their Remedies. A Special Chapter for Young Women. Worth Hundreds of Pounds.

GIVEN AWAY — **POST FREE**

40-page Up-to-Date Illustrated Catalogue of Surgical Rubber Appliances also Enclosed Free; Or with Special Sample, 2d.

A Physician writes: "This should be in the hands of every man and woman."

Call or write **P. N. HYGIENIC STORES, LTD., 95, CHARING CROSS ROAD, LONDON, W.C.** Telephone, 13,215 Central. Telegrams, Hygistor, London.

IF YOU WANT RUBBER GOODS YOU WANT THE BEST.

There is no doubt about it, common rubbish is **dear at any price**, and may cause endless expense and life-long regret that more reliable articles were not purchased.

MARVELLOUS Bargain Parcel 2/6 Containing 10 assorted samples, including the most expensive sorts. WORTH 8/-

MORRISON'S RUBBER GOODS are the **very best** obtainable, and as the demand for them is so great, they are sold at as low or even **lower prices** than are usually charged for very inferior makes. Illustrated Booklet & Sample, 2d.

SIX SPLENDID SAMPLES (assorted) ONE SHILLING (worth Treble).
The Bargain Parcel at 2/6 is offered as an advertisement for a short time only.
Packets at 2/6, 3/6, 4/6 and upwards, unequalled value.

W. MORRISON, 62 Judd Street, London, W.C.

RUBBER GOODS — SAMPLE SENT FREE.

If you want Rubber Goods you cannot do better than take advantage of this Special Offer: 12 Special Goods, 1s. 3d. Another Special Line, 2s. for 12; try a sample 6 for 1s. Our Famous XL Quality, 8d. each, 3 for 1s. 6d. Our New Finished Paragons, 1s. each; 3 for 2s.

8 Special assorted Samples 1s. The Wife's Friend, 1s. 2d. per Box of 12. Hercules Paragons (Washable), 1s., 1s. 6d., 2s. & 3s. each (everlasting wear). 12 different assorted Samples and List, including some of the best, 2s. 3d., privately packed.

NO BETTER VALUE OFFERED.

The Husband's and Wife's Malthusian Handbook, illustrated, sent absolutely Free to Adults on receipt of name and address, or with Sample Rubber Goods 2d.

Send for my Special Sample Packet of 13, containing 1 of every different kind of appliance in use, so that you will know what suits you best. Worth 10/6, sent privately for 3/6 only. Post Free.

Call or Write, **P. N. HYGIENIC STORES, Ltd., Manufacturers, 95, CHARING CROSS ROAD, LONDON,** Telephone, 13,215 Central.
(2 doors from the Palace Theatre.) Money returned if goods are not satisfactory.

LADIES! DON'T WORRY!

Send for Dr. PATTERSON'S FAMOUS FEMALE PILLS,

Which remove irregularities, Suppressions, &c., by simple means under half hour. Recommended by eminent Physicians and thousands of Ladies, being the only Genuine Remedy, and to prove the correctness of the above statement, we will send absolutely free, securely packed and free from observation, with medical certificate and testimonials, a sample packet—packet that will cure. (Send no money.) (Guaranteed genuine under a penalty of £5,000.) 2/9 Trial box 1/1 only; special extra strong, 4/3 box 2/3 only; secretly packed; guaranteed relief. (Write or Call:) Manageress, **P. N. HYGIENIC STORES, Ltd., 95, Charing Cross Rd., LONDON, W.C.** Estd. 59 years. Telephone: 13,215 Central. (Advice free by post.) Beware of dangerous Imitations. An interesting Guide for Ladies, 50 illustrations and 100 pages, also free.

PHOTOS, BOOKS, ETC.

Try the old firm. Sample Parcels.
Ripping Value, 5/-, 10/- and 20/-, or send one stamp for sample Cabinet and Catalogue Free.

A. VENENTTI, July Road, Liverpool, E.

MOUSTACHE

A nice, manly moustache Speedily Grows by using "Mousta," the guaranteed Moustache Forcer Acts like magic. Age no object. Money returned if not entirely successful. Box sent (in plain cover) for 6d. and 1d. for postage. Send 7d. to **J. D. DIXON & CO., 42, Junction Rd., London, N.**

PHOTOS.

VERY GOOD AND CLEAR FRENCH PHOTOS. Just the kind to make your friends laugh. Sample parcel 1s. 6d. Don't forget to send or you will miss a treat. **Mons. F. LEFEVRE, 2, Wood Street, Liverpool.**

FREE TO LADIES.

Our recent offer of a FREE SAMPLE of NURSE POWELL'S POPULAR PELLETS (POPLETS Regd.), met with such striking success that we have decided to repeat the offer. Ladies should write for free box enclosing stamp for postage. Delay is dangerous; write at once and obtain relief.
NURSE F. N. POWELL REMEDY CO., Wandsworth, London.

RARE BOOKS, ETC.

The Loves of a Grisette, New Translated Novel (Illustrated), 144 French Beauties, 144 Special Snapshots and our lists for 3d. Lover's Budget of Fun and Amusement, 3d. Revelations of Girlhood, 3d. Love, Courtship, and Marriage, 4d. Three Weeks, 1s. 2d. Five Nights, 1s. 2d. The Diary of a Lost One, 1s. 3d. Book of Nature, illustrated, 1s. 36 Parisian Cabinets, 6d. The Decameron, complete, 2s. Fanny Hill, 8 coloured plates, 2s. only. The Bride, illustrated with 5 plates, 5d. only. Delilah, Fair but Frail, 326 pages, 2s. Aristotle's Great Medical Works, very best edition, new and extra coloured plates, 1s. only. Anna Lombard, 1s. 2d. A Woman's Life, 1s. 2d. The Diary of My Honeymoon, 1s. 2d. A Ladies' Man, 1s. 2d. Life's Sweetest Sin, 1s. 1 Doz. Snapshot Cabinets from Life, 1s. 3 Doz., all different, 2s. 6d. Transparent Playing Cards, 2s. 6d. per Pack. Magic Revealers 4d. each, or 3 for 9d., all different. Secret Transparent Postcards 3d. and 6d. packet. A Free Gift of 360 French Beauties with each order.

SAMPLE SHEETS AND LIST SENT **FREE** TO ADULTS ONLY.

SAFE RUBBER GOODS

Our Own Manufacture. Guaranteed Reliable.

Utmost secrecy observed. 38 page list, illustrated, sent free; 6 Good Samples, 1s.; 4 Special Samples, 1s.; 10 Special Assorted 2s. (worth 6s.); 12 Special Finished Seamless, 2s. 6d., 4s., 5s., and 7s. for 12. Special Seamless (will not shrink), 2s. 9d., 4s., 6s. and 8s. for 12; Seamless Paragons, everlasting wear, 1s. 6d., 2s. 6d., and 3s. 6d. each. Our famous Hercules, 1s. each, The Dorsan Paragon, guaranteed for 1 year, 5s. each. New Samson, 7d. each, 3 for 1s. 6d. Wife's Handbook and Family Medical Guide, 80 pages, illustrated, sent free in sealed envelope, one best sample and list 2d.

P. N. DORSAN & CO., ROBSON ROAD, WEST NORWOOD, LONDON.

ADVICE TO LADIES.

If you are suffering from any diseases of the Urinary Organs, or of Suppressions and Irregularities, or any other secret ailments, we will give you advice free if you send full particulars in Confidence. Ladies can write to the Manageress (or call), **P. N. HYGIENIC STORES, Ltd., 95, Charing Cross Road, London, W.C.** (2 doors from Palace Theatre.) Tel.: 13215 Central.

RELIABLE AND GENUINE RACING NEWS.

BY AN EXPERIENCED TURFITE.

SPECIAL **SATURDAY SNIPS.**

Terms, 2s. [See page 11.

A LADY

Can recommend a remedy that simply acts like magic in curing all irregularities of female system.

NO PILLS OR MEDICINE TO TAKE.

20 years continued success speaks for itself.

Write **MRS. HILDA B. MANNERS, 2, Princeton Street, W.C.**

RUBBER GOODS

(GUARANTEED).

One price only, 1/6 for 12. Send 1/6 for 12 at once. I will buy them back for 5s. if you are not satisfied. Over 20,000 customers all over the world. Catalogue and 3 samples, 7 stamps, post free.

B. BERRY, JULY ROAD, LIVERPOOL, E.

Although not allowed to say so, many of the pills advertised for women's problems hinted that they would induce a miscarriage

69d.

an experienced maid or promiscuous daughter of a friend of the family.

William Dugdale "one of the most prolific publishers of filthy books" was born in 1800 and died 68 years later in the House of Correction. He wrote most of his own material but was not averse to stealing, plagiarising and translating the works of others and passing it off as his own. Nobody could bring a writ without incriminating themselves. His works would have such titles as "School, or Early Experiences of a Young Flagellant" supposedly written by a 'Rosa Belinda Coote'.

THE COLLECTOR; PISANUS FRAXI

Henry Spencer Ashbee was a man with a mission. After setting himself up comfortably he devoted the rest of his life to "travel, bibliography and book collecting." The books mentioned were in many cases very rare, his main interest being pornography which he collected and read from all over Europe. He left behind an invaluable guide to the kind of books available 'under the counter' in Victorian England.

Ashbee was born in London in 1834 and wrote under the pseudonym of 'Pisanus Fraxi' the surname being a derivation of the Latin for ash or ashtree. Ashbee was very thorough in his research whose aim it was to 'catalogue' as thoroughly, and at the same time, as tersely as possible, books which, as a rule, have not been mentioned by former bibliographers, and to notice them in such a way that the collector or student may be able to form a pretty just estimate of their value or purport, without having recourse to the books themselves.

Some of the varied titles summarised by Fraxi include: 'The Woman of Pleasure's Pocket Companion', containing six erotic but not indecent tales, the Dialogue between a Woman and a Virgin, this book sold for two shillings, its thirty-five pages being an explanation of the pleasures of sexual intercourse from the experienced Voluptua to the immature virgin, Lydia. The Bedfellows consists of six confidential dialogues between two

69e.

70. The fuller figure fashionable in late Victorian England.

DAMAROIDS CURE WEAK MEN.

☞ FREE OFFER ☜

25,000 FREE SAMPLE PACKETS OF "DAMAROIDS" FOR "POLICE NEWS" READERS

100,000 MEN HAVE TAKEN OUR ADVICE, WHY NOT YOU?

THIS MAN IS YOUNG AT 55 YEARS.

The secret of lifelong youth may be summed up in one word—**VITALITY**. If you have this great natural power in abundance years count for nothing. We use no electricity—we recommend none. No privations, no dieting, and no restrictions, excepting that all dissipation must cease. Take "Damaroids" and let it send its power into your nerves, organs, and blood while you are awake or sleeping. It gives you vitality. One Damaroid and you are like a new being; it takes all the pain and weakness out of your back and limbs; it makes you answer the morning greeting with "I'm feeling fine." Damaroids are the greatest strength builder; they overcome the results of earlier mistakes. They give you a **compelling power**, so that you are attractive to all with whom you come in contact. Charles L. Snell, Newport, writes:

"*I am a strong man again thanks to Damaroids. Nothing can discourage me now.*"

This is one among thousands of unsolicited testimonials.) Send for our two books, "The Secrets of Youth" and a **Free Sample Packet**, which every man should have. **Send no money.**

Call or Write **P. N. HYGIENIC STORES, LTD., LABORATORIES,**
95, Charing Cross Road, London. Telephone: Regent 823. Business Hours 9 a.m. till 12 p.m.

☞ SPECIAL 4/6 TRIAL BOX 2/3 ONLY. ☜
WHICH TAKE EFFECT IN A FEW MINUTES.

A Splendid Selection — **Every One Useful**

SEND AT ONCE FOR MY SPECIAL SAMPLE PACKET.

11 Different Kinds OF SURGICAL APPLIANCES.

THIS WONDERFUL PACKET WILL BE SENT UNDER STRICT COVER FOR

3s. 6D.
SENT FREE.
TOTAL VALUE OF ABOVE 10s.

40 page Illustrated Catalogue and Sample, 3 Stamps. These goods supplied to adults only. Call and inspect our goods.
Business Hours: 9.30 a.m. till 12 p.m.

Dept. P.N., **W. GEORGE**, 21, Green Street, Leicester Square, London, W.C.

PHOTOS.

VERY GOOD AND CLEAR FRENCH PHOTOS. Just the kind to make your friends laugh. Sample parcel 1s. 6d. Don't forget to send or you will miss a treat. Mons. F. LEFEVRE, 2, Wood Street, Liverpool.

PHOTOS, BOOKS, ETC.

Try the old firm. Sample Parcels.
Ripping Value, 5/-, 10/- and 20/-, or send one stamp for sample Cabinet and Catalogue Free.

A. VENENTTI,
July Road, Liverpool, E.

WHISKERS & MOUSTACHIOS

Positively forced to grow heavily on the smoothest face in a few weeks, no matter at what age, by using EDWARDS' INSTANTANEOUS AMERICAN HARLENE, the World-renowned Remedy for Baldness, from whatever cause arising. As a Curer of Weak and Thin Eyelashes or Restoring Grey Hair to its Original Colour it never fails. 1s. per bottle. Post free from observation. 1s. 3d. Postal Order preferred.—H. EDWARDS, 5, New Oxford street, London, W.C.

AFTER USE.

With 'everlasting' and 'washable' condoms one can only contemplate the record number of entries if the famous Guinness book had been available at the time.

MANHOOD!
HOW LOST! HOW REGAINED!
Invaluable Remarks to Young and Middle aged Men.
A CLOTH BOUND TREATISE ON WEAKNESS IN MEN: ITS CAUSE AND CURE.
5 penny stamps, write
C. 5, Gould's Laboratory, Bradford, Yorks.
Copyright] [Registered.

A RELIABLE REMEDY

FREE to Ladies

On receipt of stamped envelope I will send a Free Sample and particulars of Nurse Hammond's Improved Remedies for Ladies which act in a few hours when all else fails. Surprisingly Effective. Success Guaranteed. Address, Nurse M. Hammond, 244, High Holborn, London, W.C.

RELIABLE RUBBER GOODS.

IF U R A Y Z U L C I XL IN
THESE ARE THE BEST SEAMLESS.
Each in envelope tested and perfect.
For 12 **3/-** For 12
Why Pay More Why Pay More
New Washable Paragons 1/- each. 3 for 2/6
Ladies Rubber Appliances 1/6 each. 3 for 4/-
I will return 4 times the price for any of these goods if not satisfied. Adults Only Supplied.
Price List Free.
E. GOLDING (Manufacturer),
3, Edenbridge Rd., Hackney, London, N.E.
Call or Write. Save 50%. Established 40 years.

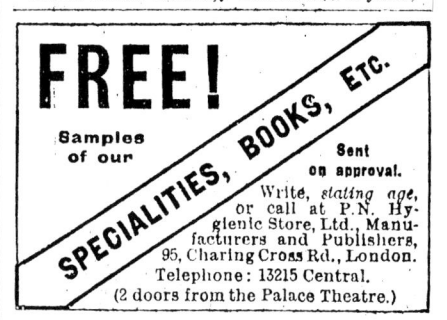

FREE!
Samples of our **SPECIALITIES, BOOKS, ETC.** Sent on approval.

Write, *stating age*, or call at P.N. Hygienic Store, Ltd., Manufacturers and Publishers, 95, Charing Cross Rd., London.
Telephone: 13215 Central.
(2 doors from the Palace Theatre.)

RARE BOOKS

A **FREE GIFT** of 144 PARISIENNES and 216 FRENCH DANCERS with each order, or a CHOICE PENDANT. Say which.

"London by Night" and 360 chic female pictures, 3d. "The Magic Revealer," magnifies 1,000 times, 4d. each, or 3 for 9d. "Love, Courtship, and Marriage," very curious, 4d. "The Parisian Dancing Girl," has real live legs, 4d. "Mysteries of a Convent," 3d. "Confessions of a Lady's Maid, or Boudoir Intrigue," beautifully illustrated, 3d. "Fanny Hill," 6d. "Adventures of a Ballet Girl," 5d. Six months in a Convent, 3d. "Startling Revelations of Girlhood," 3d. "Awful Disclosures of Maria Monk," 3d. "Sappho," the great French novel, 5d., or any four of above for 1s. Love Frolics of a Young Scamp, 1s. 6d. Secret French Transparent Postcards, 3d., 6d. and 1s. per packet. 36 Choice Parisian Cabinets, 6d. "Rosario, or the Female Monk," 1s. 6d. "The Bride," 156 pages, 5d. "The Decameron," 2s. "Aristotle's Works," 9d. and 1s. 6d. "Book of Nature," 1s. The "Heptameron," 1s. 4d. "Rhoderick Random," 1s. "Moll Flanders," 9d. Transparent Playing Cards, 2s. 6d. a pack. 8 Special Rubber Goods, 1s.

P.N. GOLD & Co., Prospect House, West Green, London.

SAFE RUBBER GOODS
"FOR EITHER SEX."
BEST AND CHEAPEST.

Postal department under principal's personal supervision. Utmost secrecy observed. REMEMBER Cheap Goods are dear at any price. 36 page illustrated list Sent Free, or 8 Good Samples, 1/-.
4 Perfect Samples 1/-. 6 Specials 1s. 10 Excellent Samples, including some of the best examples, 2/- (value 7/-). Our Famous New Samson 7d. each or 3 for 1/6. Best English make 2/- and 2/6 for 12. New Finished Paragons, 1/-, 1/6, 2/-, and 3/- each. Everlasting wear. Our Famous New Gossamer, 6 for 2/6. Our Famous Hercules 1/- each, 8/- for 12. Adults only supplied.
ALL GOODS BY RETURN. NO WAITING.

The Husband's and Wife's Malthusian Handbook, illustrated, sent absolutely Free to Adults on receipt of name and address, or with one best rubber sample, 2d. Book of Nature, wonderfully illustrated, 1s.

P. N. CHARLES & CO.,
MANUFACTURERS,
West Green Road, Tottenham, London.
(23 Years Advertisers in this Paper.)

budding beauties, Lucy and Kate, who tell each other their love adventures each evening when they go to bed.

The style of writing varied, with some authors deliberately using foul language to shock the reader, whilst others used the kind of expressions still found today. In the 'Amatory Experiences of a Surgeon' the medical man has abandoned himself to a life of debauchery. Here he describes one of his early conquests of a young girl:

> "I carefully raised up her clothes. As I proceeded I unveiled beauties enough to bring the dead to life, and losing all regard to delicacy, I threw them over the bosom of the sweet girl...Everything now lay bare before me, her mossy recess, shaded by only the slightest silky down, presented to my view two fully pouting lips of coral hue, while the rich swell of her lovely thighs served still further to inflame me."

A typical trailer for a book and its contents is printed below. Anything French was considered risque so titles such as 'La Rose d'Amour' were fairly common, although this particular novel was first published in the U.S.A.

> "...this hero ravishes, seduces, and ruins all the females that come within his reach - rich and poor, gentle and simple, rough and refined, all fall down before his sceptre of flesh, his noble truncheon, his weapon of war. His great passion is for maidenheads, for young and unfledged virgins...He travels the sea for new victims of his raging lust; he buys maidenheads by the score, he initiates them in all the mysteries of Venus and finally returns to his chateau with a seraglio of beauties...Every page is a picture of sensual delights, and the book is illustrated with sixteen coloured designs equal to the text. It is in two volumes and the price is three guineas."

Despite the promise of a plethora of explicit sexual adventures with a wide variety of partners in exotic locations not all books lived up to their billing.

'Intrigues and Confessions of a Ballet Girl' was just that and would today be rejected by girls' magazines, not for being too racy, but too dull. Prices fell with improved technology and by 1913 saucy books were being advertised in papers such as the Illustrated Police News, though whether the products lived up to their billing is extremely doubtful. Buyers were offered '360 pretty Paris girls free with each order'.

FOUR THOUSAND PAGES OF ANONYMOUS SEXUAL MEMOIRS

The most famous English pornographic book to surface in the last century was undoubtedly, 'My Secret Life.' Famous not for the reasons of being well-written or erotic, but because the book consists of eleven volumes detailing the anonymous author's sex life, and whoever he was he was certainly a man possessed.

'My Secret Life' is of interest because it is a unique document of sexual morals in the Victorian age, and today is very rare. It was published in 1888 and contains over 4,000 pages. The author was probably in his sixties at the time of publication and had been trying to get the work into print for several years. The author made a note in his diary of his sexual encounters and would write them up in complete detail a few days later.

Several of the writer's experiences take place in London; here he describes a trip to the docks:

> 'As we walked outside, I saw a number of stout, vulgar looking, flamingly dressed women without bonnets, some in twos – some alone – some with sailors – talking bawdily and openly in the public streets. It was to me quite a new phase of London life...
>
> My friend knew sailors' necessities, and their habits, and those of their female acquaintances ashore, for he was a large ship owner... To amuse me and satisfy my curiosity, we dined together a few days afterwards, and after our dinner, visited several of the public houses. To avoid remark and possibly offensive behaviour towards us, we dressed in the shabbiest possible manner, and with caps bought just opposite the docks, and such as were worn largely by the working people in the neighbourhood, we flattered ourselves that we looked as common a couple of men as ever barrows along the street.
>
> Thus costumed we spent the evening at public houses, among sailors, whores, and working men – in an atmosphere thick and foul with tobacco smoke, sweat and gas. We ordered liquors which we threw under the table or spilt when not observed; we treated some gay women, but in a very modest way, and altogether had a very entertaining evening. It was difficult to act up to our disguise. We asked the women to bet which of us had the biggest prick, and the girls felt us outside quite openly. There was, however, nothing likely to shock people there. Of lewd talk there was plenty, though no gross indecency was practised. The barmen, or potboys, or the master were always there and checked it "Now you Sally, none of that; or out you go." – "Now hook it smart you bitch," were phrases we heard with others, used by the master or servants when things got too hot.'

The anonymous author gave himself the pseudonym Walter. If one reads between the lines of sexual conquest few books reveal in such detail the lives of working women:

> "The angle of the street named as leading out of the Strand was dark of a night and a favourite place for doxies to go to relieve their bladders. The police took no notice of such trifles, provided it was not done on the greater thoroughfare (although I have seen at night women do it openly in the gutters of the Strand); in the particular street I have seen them pissing almost in rows; yet they most usually went in twos to do that for a woman likes a screen, one usually standing up till the other has finished, and then taking her turn. Indeed the pissing in all bye-streets of the Strand is continuous."

The author seemed to show a keen interest in the girls whose services he employed. Kitty's reasons for prostituting herself must have been similar to those of tens of thousands of women in Victorian England:

The Days' Doings.

An Illustrated Journal of Romantic Events, Reports, Sporting & Theatrical News at Home & Abroad.

Vol. II.—No. 48.] PUBLISHED AT No. 300, STRAND, LONDON, W.C.—SATURDAY, JUNE 24, 1871. [PRICE THREEPENCE.

AWKWARD CONTRE-TEMPS IN REGENT STREET DURING THE HEIGHT OF THE SEASON.
"That Girl seems to know you, George!"

70a. Most readers got their scandal, gossip and titillation from illustrated magazines.

"She said, 'I buy things to eat; I can't eat what mother gives us. She is poor, and works very hard; she'd give us more, but she can't; so I buy foods, and gives the others what mother gives me; they don't know no better - I eat some; sometimes we have only gruel and salt; if we have a fire we toast the bread, but I can't eat it if I am not dreadfully hungry.'

'What do you like?'

'Pies and sausage-rolls,' said the girl smacking her lips and laughing. Oh! my eye, ain't that prime, - oh!'

'That's what you went gay for!'

'I'm not gay' said she sulkily

'Well what you let men fuck you for?'

'Yes.'

'Sausage-rolls.'

'Sausage-rolls and pastry too.'"

Little has changed in the male anxiety stakes. Well over one hundred years ago Walter was wondering whether his matrimonial peace-maker stood comparison with other members of the male sex. Who better to ask than the doxies whose company he sought to indulge in his favourite pastime?

"When they said it was a very good size - as big as most - I did not believe them, and I used when I pulled it out to say in an apologetic tone. 'Let's put it up, there's not much of it.' Oh! it's quite big enough', one would say. 'I've seen plenty smaller.'"

There was no shortage of wit and humour in the age of Oscar Wilde. One of thousands of anonymous Victorian limericks is quoted below.

There was a young fellow named Bliss
Whose sex life was strangely amiss
For even with Venus
His recalcitrant penis
Would never do better than t
                          h
                           i
                            s

One can imagine Oscar himself uttering the following off-the-cuff remark: "Bigamy is having one wife too many...monogamy is the same!" (anon).

Only a relatively small number of Victorians actually saw or read much pornography.

With the marked improvement in literacy towards the end of the century an increased demand for information was met by a number of illustrated magazines which dealt with human interest stories. Titles such as 'The Day's Doings' reported on 'romantic events' whilst other specialised publications dealt with more intimate problems.

'DELICATE NELL' AND 'SPOTS ON FACE'

The 'Family Doctor' answered readers questions free of charge. Sufferers would write in using a pseudonym detailing their complaints; advice would be offered in the next issue. The one problem for today's readers is that the complaint was not listed, only the magazine's solution. One can only guess as to the problem from the advice given, which, today, would not look out of place in a satirical magazine, but in 1886 was deadly serious.

Those with questions wrote under such pseudonyms as 'Half Dead; Anxious and Worried One; Anxious Nancy; Dicky Sam; Tortured; Delicate Nell and Spots on Face.'

Most were told to wash in cold water, take exercise and cut down on drinking and smoking. Others were advised as follows:

To a Reader: 'You must give it up at once or else we cannot do you any good. The books you mention are written either by or for quacks to frighten young men. You need not alarm yourself, but must follow our instructions. Avoid all stimulating drinks and food. No supper.'

To Volo non Valeo: 'We think you should leave them off, for if they make you faint you may be quite sure they do not suit you. Take a cold bath every morning and a hot one once a week.'

To Jas Barrett: 'They must be cut out.'

To One in a Fix: 'We think the left side is the best.'

To Out of Work: 'Quite natural. Do not smoke. Take iron and quinine three times a day, and the less courting you do the better, particularly if you are out of work.'

To Elsie: 'You probably know the cause of this better than we do.'

To A Hill: 'Take a long rest.'

To Mantis: 'We think you had better put yourself under the care of an experienced physician. Morphia habitues cannot undertake their cure themselves as a rule.'

To Curiosity: 'We do not give advice on the subject of your letter, and we are very much surprised you write to a respectable paper about such matters, but we will not jump down your throat.'

To Nemo: 'No, you have nothing to fear at all, only don't do it again!'

To M.J.D. Hirwain: 'We do not give any advice on this subject; the only thing to do is to make you marry him at once.'

To a Little Welsh Girl: 'No it will not; the juice of fresh lemons only.'

To an Inquirer: 'It is quite time you gave it up; you cannot always expect to be young. Take quinine and iron (Lorimer's) three times a day. You should not have married a woman so much younger than yourself, the idea is not right, it is only the voice of Nature.'

'FULL OF STRANGE OATHS'

FIRKYTOODLING AND FLYING PASTIES: HISTORICAL SLANG

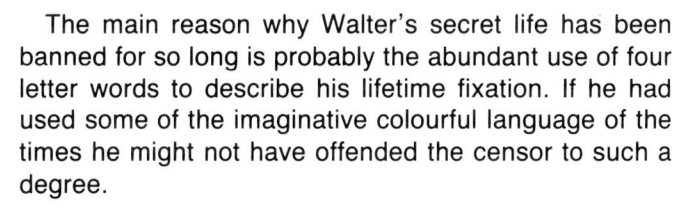

*71. Now you see it,
One of the first saucy postcards.*

now you don't.

The main reason why Walter's secret life has been banned for so long is probably the abundant use of four letter words to describe his lifetime fixation. If he had used some of the imaginative colourful language of the times he might not have offended the censor to such a degree.

Instead of what appears to be Walter's favourite word for coition he might have invited his female friends to: "do the matrimonial polka," "wriggle navels," "join paunches," "play pickle-me-tickle-me" or "do the mattress-jig."

The slang dictionary has over one hundred words for vulva, though most of them, being invented by men, might still give offence today.

Breasts might be referred to as: "a dumpling shop," "an apple-dumpling shop," "baby's public-house," "cupids kettle-drums," "the milky-way," "coker-nuts" and "bubbles."

Synonyms for penis included: "live rabbit," "rhubarb" (how's your rhubarb coming up, Bill?), "rolling-pin," "silent flute," "Hampton wick," "nebuchadnezzar," "old Adam," "Julius Caesar," "key," "matrimonial peacemaker," "broomstick," "catso," "credentials," "dearest member," "the best leg of three," "club," "Doctor Johnson," "baby-maker," "bean," "beef," "belly ruffian," "bald-headed hermit," "barber's sign," "star-gazer," "sugar-stick" and "gardener."

There were several colourful expressions relating to sex which cannot be easily classified. 'To fight in armour' would indicate that a condom was worn during intercourse. To 'lie in state' meant to sleep with two or three women. If you were asked to 'sling a slobber' this was a request for a kiss but you would have to watch out for a 'horse-kiss' which was an intended kiss that turned into a bite. Kissing was also commonly referred to as 'Jowl-sucking, which might lead to a bout of firkytoodling (heavy petting). It's hard to imagine someone asking 'do you fancy a quick firkytoodle?'

Girls had quick replies to the verbal attacks sometimes received on the streets. To the oft asked question: "Does your mother know you're out?" The answer was 'Yes she gave me a farthing to buy a monkey, are you for sale?' To the accusation 'You're cracked' would come back the reply 'Yes but in the right place.' If a girl asked the time the reply was often 'Half past kissing time and time to kiss again.'

If a woman was married to a sour apple-tree (married to a bad-tempered husband) she would have to be careful he did not give her the key to the street (turn her out of home). A so-called 'cockney luxury' in the days of outside privvies was 'breakfast in bed and a shit in the pot.'

Anyone who was eccentric was said to 'have maggots in the head' and those a little slow to catch on 'have no milk in the coconut'. Weak beer was known as arms and legs, it having no body.

Finally, a word of warning: Flying pasties and buttered buns are not for consumption!

Boat journeys seem to change the behaviour and habits of the normal polite and sober Londoner.

As the Brits make straight for the bar today once they board one of the cross-Channel ferries, no matter what time of night or day, so the effect of travelling on the Thames changed the character of those engaged on the journeys, with passengers and boatmen hurling abuse at passing boats. It appeared that any form of insult could be hurled without rebuke and the old river had its own laws, even the royal family were insulted, which if the offence had taken place on land might have led to a charge of treason. Some of the fruity greetings have been recorded:

A scoundrel crew of Lambeth gardeners attack'd us . . . one of them beginning with us after this manner:

> 'You couple of treacherous sons of Bridewell bitches who are pimps to your own mothers, and cock-bawds[1] to the rest of your relations, who were begot by huffling[2] and christen'd out of a _____, how dare you show your ugly faces on the river of Thames?'

To which our well-fed pilot, after he had cleared his voice with a Hem, most manfully reply'd':

> "You lousie starv'd crow of worm-pickers and snail-catchers; you off-spring of a dunghill and brothers to a pumpkin, who can't afford butter to your cabbage or bacon to your sprouts; you _____ rogues, who _____. Hold your tongues, you nitty radish-mongers, or I'll whet my needle upon my _____ and sew your lips together."

This verbal engagement was no sooner over, but another squabbling crew met us, being most women, who, as they past us, gave us another salutation, viz:

> "You tailors! Who pawn'd the gentleman's cloak to buy a wedding-dinner, and afterwards sold his wife's clothes for money to fetch it out again? Here Timothy,[3] fetch your mistress and I three ha'porth of boil'd beef, see first they make good weight, then stand hard for a bit of carrot."

To which our Orator, after a puff and a pull-up being well-skill'd in the water-dialect, made this return:

> "You dirty _____ brood of night-walkers and shop-lifters, which of you was it that ty'd her apron about her neck, because she would be kissing a night-rail; and reckon'd her gallant a shilling for _____. Have a care of your cheeks you whores, we shall have you branded next sessions that the world may see your trade in your faces. You are lately come from hemp and hammer. O Good Sir Robert, knock; pray Good Sir Robert, knock."

The next board we met was freighted with a parcel of city shop-keepers, who, being eager, like the rest, to show their acuteness of wit, and admirable breeding, accosted us after this manner viz:

> "You affidavit scoundrels, pluck the straws out of the heels of your shoes. You Oats journeymen, who are you going to swear out of an estate at Westminster Hall, though you know nothing of the matter? You rogues, we shall have you in the pillory when rotten eggs are plenty. You are in a safe condition, you may travel anywhere by water and never fear drowning."

Thus they run on till our spokesman stopp'd their mouths with this following homily:

> You cuckoldy company of whiffling, peddling, lying, over-reaching ninny-hammers, who were forced to desire some handsome bachelor to kiss your wives and beg a holiday for you, or else you would not have dared to come out today — go make haste home, that you may find fowls at the fire. If I had as many horns on my head as you are forc'd to hide in your pockets, what a monster should I be? You little think what your wives are providing for you against your come home. Don't be angry friends, it's many a honest man's fortune . . .

The journey down to Greenwich is a little more tanquil these days.

[1] A cock-bawd was a man keeping a brothel.
[2] A huffle is a piece of bestiality too filthy even for early slang dictionaries.
[3] A Timothy was the old name for a child's penis.

BAWDY BALLADS

A good knowledge of sexual slang could be guaranteed after singing some of the bawdy ballads so popular in the nineteenth century.

Although the audience were 'crowded together like the Black Hole in Calcutta' and the air thick with smoke, the Coal Hole and the Cider cellars were two of the capital's main attractions in early Victorian days. The food was plain; sausages and mash, poached eggs and kidneys. The drink unexceptional; brandy, sherry, stout and punch. The attraction was the atmosphere created by the singing of bawdy ballads to the accompaniment of an old piano. Only men attended these drinking halls and many of the audience were made up from the lawyers and journalists working in the city. The landlord would act as chairman of proceedings which became more professional as news of the popularity of the evenings spread.

THE POOL OF LONDON AND TOWER BRIDGE, LONDON.

72. *The River, scene of many a verbal battle using the coarsest of language.*

73. The illustrations of song sheets left little to the imagination.

THE HEDGER AND DITCHER AND HIS NOTHING AT ALL

Air — Nothing at All.

Miss Deborah Dainty, just aged thirty-three,
Determin'd at last that she married would be,
Selected the first man that came in her way,
Which was Roger, a hedger and ditcher, they say.
Her thoughts were on fire the whole of the night,
He thought of her money, she thought of delight.
But, lord! the delight that came to her was small,
They were wed, went to bed, and did — nothing at all.

Fooral, &c.

Roger snor'd like a top, though she nudg'd him and sighed,
And "don't you snore so," very fondly she cried:
Then she kissed him, and teased him with amorous play,
But Roger turn'd over, and still snor'd away.
Then she pinch'd him, and pull'd him, until he awoke,
He grumbled, while she to him thus kindly spoke,
"Now, pray, do, do something," "I will," he did bawl.
"Ah, will ye? well, what?" "Why — do nothing at all."

Fooral, &c.

Now Roger still slept, and the maiden still whined,
And said that her spouse was to nothing inclined;
Then bade both the world and her pleasures adieu,
Pinch'd his ribs, call'd him fool, and went to sleep too,
She dreamt of joy which she then did not feel,
And on only a vision of love made a meal,
She long'd for something, though ever so small,
But he, stupid lout, long'd for nothing at all.

Fooral, &c.

When a week in this way they had murder'd or more,
Her wonder and passion were roused, to be sure;
And so she determin'd, what might come to pot,
To find if he something or nothing had got.
Curiosity prompting, one night, when he snor'd,
The source of her sorrow she quickly explor'd,
And saw quite enough forth her sorrow to call,
She looked, and she look'd, and saw nothing at all.

Fooral, &c.

In despair from her husband next morning she fled,
And into a river jumpt souse overhead,
And there she remain'd with the fishes below,
Till death in compassion had finish'd her woe.
But her spirit, they say, has not felt sorrow's rod,
For courted it was by a monstrous great cod;
I can't say it's true, so the tale I'll not maul,
But I know that she died, and for — nothing at all.

'THEY HAVE THEIR ENTRANCES AND THEIR EXITS'

Harper's New Monthly Magazine in 1891 sent a reporter to one of the capital's cheaper but very popular music halls:

"There are no dress-coats and caped cloaks, no dashing toilets, to be seen here; but the vast majority are in easy circumstances and eminently respectable. You will see little family parties — father, mother and perhaps a grown-up daughter or a child or two — in the stalls. Most of them are probably regular visitors, and have the entree here in return for exhibiting bills in their shop-windows; and these family parties all know one another, as can be seen from the smiles and handshakes they exchange as they pass in or out. Then there are several girls with their sweethearts, respectable young couples employed in neighbouring workshops and factories, and a rusty old matron or two, while the fringe of the audience is made up of gay young clerks, the local 'bloods', who have a jaunty fashion in some districts of wearing a cigar behind the ear. Large ham sandwiches are handed round by the cooks in white blouses, and when a young woman desires to be very stylish indeed, she allows her swain to order a port for her refreshment . . .

"After a song and some feats by a troupe of acrobats, came an exhibition by a young lady in a glass tank filled with water. She was a very pretty and graceful young lady, and she came on accompanied by a didactic gentleman in evening dress, who accompanied the announcement of each new feature of her performance by a little discourse. 'Opening and shutting the mouth under water,' he would say, for example. 'It has long been a theory among scientific men that by opening the mouth while under water, a vacuum is created, thereby incurring the risk of choking the swimmer. Miss So-and-so, ladies and gentlemen, will now proceed to demonstrate the fallacy of that opinion, by opening and shutting her mouth several times in succession while remaining at the bottom of the tank,' which Miss So-and-so accordingly did to our great edification. Then came 'gathering shells under water,' which was accomplished in a highly elaborate manner, so that there could be no mistake about it. 'Sewing' and 'writing under water.' 'Eating under water,' when the lady consumed a piece of bread with every appearance of extreme satisfaction. 'Drinking from a bottle under water. Most of you,' remarked the manager, sympathetically, 'are acquainted with the extreme difficulty of drinking from a bottle under any circumstances.' Then a cigar was borrowed from the audience, lighted and given to the lady, who, shielding it with her hands, retired under the water and smoked vigorously for a minute or two, reappearing with the cigar still unextinguished. Lastly the manager announced, 'Ladies and gentlemen, Miss So-and-so will now adopt the position of prayer;' whereupon the lady sank gracefully on her knees underwater, folded her hands, and appeared rapt in devotion, while the orchestra played 'the Maiden's Prayer,' and the manager, with head reverently bent, stood delicately aside, as one who felt himself unworthy to intrude upon such orisons. Then the lady adopted a pose even more imploring, and a ray, first of crimson and then of green light, was thrown into the tank, presumably to indicate morning and evening prayer respectively. After some minutes of this, the fair performer, a little out of breath from her spiritual exertions, rose, sleek and dripping, to the surface, hopped nimbly out, and bowed herself off . . ."

74. Crowding to the Pit.

As with the Valentine's cards, many music hall songs were extremely offensive and might be considered an antiaphrodisiac:

> Her beauty and praise I mean to disclose,
> She's dirty and lazy with a short stuffy nose,
> She's a disgrace to the women wherever she goes
> And her clothes all in tatters are hanging,
> With a beard on her lip like a wandering Jew,
> Not a tooth in her head that is sound only two,
> And a shift on her back neither black white or blue
> That never was wet with a washing.

> We met beside the mountain stream,
> Damp tulips deck'd her chalk white brow
> Her voice was like the night owl's scream,
> Her eyes — alas! I see them now!
> Her eyes look'd purple in the sun,
> Her teeth — they were a guinea set,
> Her age! she was but forty-one;
> She weighed but sixteen stone — and — yet
>   I could not say I loved her,
>   Nor bid her join my lot,
>   I could not say I loved her,
>   I tried — but no! could not.

> We met once more 'neath gas-light glare,
> Amid the fierce and wild quadrille.
> She was — they said — a millionaire,
> I spoke — her answer haunts me still.
> She lisp'd "I'm Thine. Wealth, beauty, all,
> My income's twenty-five pounds ten,
> We'll live near gaswork at Vauxhall,
> Say, dost thou love me now? — and then —"
>   I could not say I loved her,
>   Nor bid her join my lot,
>   I could not say I loved her,
>   I tried — but no! could not.

THE FINE LINE BETWEEN SUCCESS AND FAILURE

Jenny was deserted by her acrobat husband whilst still in her teens. With a young baby to feed she was desperate for work. Her father had encouraged her to sing in the Dr. Johnson Tavern at night whilst making paper flowers in a factory by day; later apprenticed to a publican who stayed open until two o'clock every morning; Jenny, besides serving ale, had to be ready to sing at a moment's notice if so requested by a customer. Rising at five o'clock every day to polish, scrub and bottle beer she was in danger of aging before her time. Jenny made her way to London with the express intent of getting a break in the difficult and competitive world of music hall.

Pestering all the theatrical agents was the only way she knew how but none would take any notice of the poor bedraggled girl. Near to starvation she persisted in her efforts to find work and every day waylaid one of the most important agents until he begrudgingly wrote her a letter to take to a Mr. Loibl at the London Pavillion. He let Jenny know that there might be a job as an extra but promised nothing more. Passing her young baby onto a poor friend she ran to the showhouse and asked for her note to be given to the aforementioned Mr. Loibl who soon appeared with a perplexed look on his face. Who was this young lady still recovering her strength as she related her previous experience?

Jenny's luck changed, she was offered a small slot on the bill before the famous 'Champagne Charlie,' George Leybourne. Despite not having eaten, Jenny gave her all, she caught their attention, she held their attention. She was alive, dynamic, her eyes shone with the pleasure of performing, Jenny finished her song but the crowd would not let her go, they had forgotten their beer and chops and were shouting for 'encore' after 'encore' until "The Vital Spark" could do no more. Leybourne ran onto the stage and lifted the new star into the air.

Having not eaten during the day she feasted on champagne in the evening. Jenny would go on to sing five or six songs, do male impersonations and dance delightfully over the next few years.

She bought herself a large house and toured the States before being forced to retire due to ill-health. What was in the letter from the agent to Mr. Loibl that might have saved Jenny's life? He showed it to her after her first performance:

> "Don't trouble to see the bearer. I have simply sent her up to get rid of her. She's troublesome.
> Yours . . ."

TURTLE-RIDING IN THE AUSTRALIAN OUTBACK

Louis de Rougemont claimed to be an explorer. Arriving in London he related his travels in the remote areas of Northern Australia in "Wide World Magazine". Victorians were used to reading daring tales of adventure in dark continents but some of Louis's stories were a little difficult to believe. Readers might have swallowed tales of gold as large as boulders lying in the desert. When he started recalling seeing winged animals a few readers were becoming sceptical. He then claimed that he chanced upon two white maidens living in the wilderness. Few sensible people now believed his story yet he persisted in telling tales of how he crossed the swift flowing rivers (as we now know there are no such rivers). Louis de Rougemont stated that he crossed these natural barriers in a most original manner. He confided that he had mounted on the shells of huge turtles which were abundant, and placing one foot on either side of their head guided them the way he wanted to go.

75. Taken Places Occupied.

The Hippodrome theatre decided to put these facts to the test and built a large water tank and provided the necessary turtles. De Rougemont was not the type of person to flinch from a challenge and with a packed house on the first night he mounted his first turtle. These creatures were not quite so obliging as the ones he had met in the outback as each time they went into the water they proceeded to submerge leaving the story-teller to swim to the sides. The audiences kept coming however and on one day he did manage to hold on most of the way across the pool before being thrown. Louis de Rougemont claimed this one partial success proved he had been telling the truth all along.

The Hippodrome often made use of its water tank to take the audience on trips to far-off lands. Dogs were made up to look like wolves and a whole Siberian adventure acted out terminating with sledge and horses plunging into the water to escape their tormentors.

Fox hunts with hounds and huntsmen swimming a river were followed by a show with Redskins shooting rapids and shows such as 'The Earthquake' and 'The Typhoon' succeeded in making the audience feel quite sea-sick.

THEATRICAL PLEASURES. PL.3.

London Pub.d by Tho.s M.c Lean, 26. Haymarket.

76. *Snug in the Gallery.*

'ALL THE WORLD'S A STAGE'

THE O.P. RIOTS

One of the most original and successful campaigns of civil disobedience began in the theatre in 1809. The previous year Covent Garden theatre had been burnt down and to offset the cost of rebuilding and refurbishment the management determined to raise prices. The increase was not extortionate but enraged the local patrons who determined to force the theatre to charge the old admission prices. On the management side John Kemble was held to be responsible and as he appeared on the opening night he was greeted with hisses, yells, catcalls and the blowing of horns. The audience succeeded in drowning his every speech.

To show there was no animosity towards the actors these would be cheered but in such volume as they could not be heard. The ringleaders would then stand with their back to the stage and start to distribute leaflets highlighting their grievances. This was followed by the entire audience moving in a slow and rhythmic manner in what was to become known as the "O.P." (old price) dance. They would beat sticks and shout "O.P." to every beat.

Kemble realising that he would never be heard went into print to try and justify the price rises but his arguments were dismissed out of hand. Even when he resorted to the full weight of the law, charging the ringleaders in court with incitement to riot, the case was dismissed. The actors continued to take the stage every night even though not one word could be heard. It was common to see missiles flying through the air and across the stage and the odd body would go the same way as rioters and those trying to maintain order clashed all over the theatre. These scenes carried on relentlessly for a full sixty-one nights before Kemble finally gave in and lowered the prices to their old level.

The very next day all trouble ceased and the patrons enjoyed the evenings performance as if nothing out of order had ever occurred.

PENN'ORTHS OF PICCALILLI AT THE PENNY PLAYHOUSE

Let us join the correspondent of 'The Million' on a trip to a Whitechapel penny playhouse one hundred years ago:

"The room is a large one, capable of seating between four and five hundred people. It is lit up by a huge chandelier from the centre. The chandelier once was the joy of a prominent provincial music hall.

Here are tailors, cigar makers, cap makers, watch-makers and even an occasional diamond polisher. Many of them are respectable-looking young fellows whose wages are small and will not permit of a too expensive theatrical indulgence. The women are in strong force, dressed as one of them expressed it on the entrance of a certain lady in black satin and beaded trimming — "up to the knocker." Many of the young girls are very pretty — some of them handsome. They are all workers in the factories, with which the East End abounds — cigarette-makers, artificial florists, millinery workers &c — and here they meet, compare fashions as keenly and criticise the others as closely as the occupants of the boxes at the opera. An occasional baby sometimes makes its appearance and the wrath of the audience knows no bounds. "Put it under the seat," "Turn it out," "Give it a dose of Laudanum," and other expressive epithets are hurled at the mother of the boisterous baby until the child is removed.

Beer and refreshments are sold, but the eatables are distinctly better than the drinkables. Hollands is the favourite liquid, and you can get a pennyworth of whisky. Three waiters are kept busily employed all the evening. The eatables are set out on a separate table. These consist of sandwiches at 1d each, fried fish and bread at 1½d, and a huge basin containing a great delicacy hereabouts — pickled cucumber. One must not forget three or four good sized jars of pickles at the back — piccalilli, a sort of mustard pickle in which all kinds of vegetables appear — is always in demand, "penn'orths" being served out in saucers.

And so a busy trade is kept up all night, the bar being presided over by a gentleman with remarkably big, black, bushy whiskers, who is assisted by a little girl who washes up. The stage is a fair size though the stock of scenery is limited. The properties — such as chairs, tables, or any other article of furniture required are often lent by those taking part. The audience is not exacting in the way of scenery. It wants acting, and plenty of it. The cost of performances — some of which last five and six hours — averages out a penny a time. There are a few actors who get paid; at the most five shillings a night and then he must be a "star" and capable of filling the house.

The audience, for boisterous excitement and extravagant encouragement would be hard to equal. Nothing will upset them. They possess the kindest souls in creation. Young Ponsonby may forget his part; the beautiful Miss Grace Cherrystone may trip over her train; or some important actor may not turn up, and an obliging young Roscius walks on and reads it out of the book. It is all right and good humour reigns supreme.

The orchestra consists of a piano. This is presided over by a lady who has been known to play for two hours at a stretch owing to something being wrong behind the scenes. And so they go on until the curtain is ready to rise, talking fashion and eating penn'orths of piccalilli, discussing the probabilities of the last drop of whisky they had being watered.

Hush! The bell is heard tinkling behind. There is a sound of rushing at the back, and the audience pull themselves together to witness a representation of the "Two Orphans", for which a friend of one of the waiters has lent a real knife-grinding machine as he happens to possess one. A big "S-s-sh-sh-sh" goes through the hall, the piano goes "bang", the roller of the curtain is seen to totter, the canvas rolls slowly and laboriously up, there is a frantic roar of applause, a voice is heard from the wings — evidently that of the prompter — which says, "Now, then, get on." The youth addressed nervously enters; more applause, another bang on the "band" s-s-sh-sh-sh the performance has commenced!

THEATRICAL PLEASURES. Pl. 2.

77. *Contending for a Seat.*

78. Robert Coates, as Romeo would offer snuff to the audience.

'DIE AGAIN ROMEO'

The theatre has long been one of the main attractions to London and has provided innumerable stories of success and failure. Robert Coates was probably the most eccentric and unlikely star to tread the boards on the London stage. His rise to fame at the age of thirty-six was totally unexpected as he had no talent whatsoever. His face was much wrinkled and he seemed to be wearing a permanent cunning grin. He was known for his odd dress sense, sporting heavy fur coats whatever the weather and diamond buttons on his waistcoat and buckles on his shoes. He was the most unlikely of people ever to be cast as Romeo in an amateur production in Bath.

He took the stage wearing a cloak of sky-blue silk, covered with spangles. This was complemented by red pantaloons and an opera hat sat upon a large wig. The pantaloons were much too tight and through a rip his shirt protruded throughout much of the play. All of his lines were uttered in coarse tones.

Captain Gronow was present and takes up the story:

> 'The balcony scene was interrupted by shrieks of laughter, for in the midst of one of Juliet's impassioned exclamations, Romeo quietly took out his snuff-box and applied a pinch to his nose; on this a wag in the gallery bawled out, "I say, Romeo, give us a pinch," when the impassioned lover in the most affected manner, walked to the side boxes and offered the contents of his box first to the gentlemen and then with great gallantry to the ladies . . . Romeo then returned to the balcony, and was seen to extend his arms; but all passed in dumb show, so incessant were the shouts of laughter . . .

> The dying scene was irresistibly comic, for Romeo dragged the unfortunate Juliet from the tomb, much in the same manner as a washerwoman throws in her cart the bag of foul linen. But how shall I describe his death? Out came a dirty silk handkerchief from his pocket, with which he carefully swept the ground; this his opera hat was carefully placed for a pillow, and down he laid himself. After various tossings about, he seemed reconciled to his position; but the house vociferously bawled "Die again, Romeo" and obedient to the command, he rose up and went through the ceremony again."

> Juliet quickly brought the play to a close as Romeo was contemplating his third death.

Mistakenly encouraged by the applause Robert Coates took to the London stage but after a certain initial interest he was forced to seek the attention he craved by driving along the capital's streets in a barouche designed like at cockle-shell and drawn by two milk-white steeds.

PARLIAMENT SUSPENDED SO M.P.s MAY WITNESS ANOTHER ACTOR AT WORK

Child stars are certainly not a phenomenom of the twentieth century. The fourteen year old Master William Betty, the Infant Roscius, was responsible for an incredible demand for seats. By the time he arrived in London in the early 1800s he could earn between fifty and one hundred pounds per performance. His sole attraction seems to have been his good looks and such was his reputation that theatre-goers would attempt to hide under their seats after the previous evening's performance. Parliament was suspended so that the M.P.s could see another actor at work. The audience would gather very early in the morning and on one occasion a crowd broke down the doors and smashed windows just to see the pretty young boy. William used to play Romeo or Hamlet and soon amassed a fortune of thirty thousand pounds before retiring at the age of seventeen. A short-lived comeback at the age of twenty-two increased his funds but he was now rather awkward and his voice was not what it had been. Few people can claim to have lived for sixty years after retirement but the Infant Roscius died unknown towards the latter end of the nineteenth century.

79. Master William Betty the child prodigy and stage sensation in the early 1800's.

Two other performances worth a mention in this section. George Cooke (1756-1812) was too drunk to play the lead in 'Love à la mode' and the show was presented without him or an understudy in his place. Earlier this century Noel Coward's 'Sirocco' was booed for a full ten minutes after the curtain fell, nonetheless the leading actress Frances Doble gave a curtain-speech stating that it was the happiest day of her life!

LONDON BY NIGHT

Dance Halls is perhaps too grandiose a word for the basements of taverns near the docks. They did have one big attraction, however, they were free. Sailors from all corners of the globe interested in wine, women and song, though not necessarily in that order were the main customers. Ratcliffe Highway was the principal attraction as there was an abundance of taverns with rooms for dancing and singing. Amongst the most famous were Paddy's Goose, the Prussian Flag and the Pickled Herring.

James Greenwood's description of an evening at the Prussian Flag in 1870:

> "There was a long room with a resplendent bar at one end, and at the other the "orchestra" — four street musicians, who wore their hats or caps, and smoked clay pipes between the items. The women, before dancing, removed their hats and hung them on a row of hooks. All were dressed in silk or satin, with bare arms and shoulders, and all of them were hard-faced and hard-voiced. The men, most of whom were drunk, were seafaring men of all countries — Italians, Germans, African negroes, Americans, Britons, and men from the East, brown, copper-coloured, and yellow. Some of them danced in sea-boots; some of them, for greater agility, removed coat and waistcoat. But everything was orderly.
>
> Four hefty young bruisers attended to that. They moved about the room coatless, with shirt-sleeves rolled back, showing their biceps. They acted as waiters, but their real job was to keep order, and to see that no robbery or fight happened on the premises. What happened off the premises was no concern of theirs. They would stop two girls from trying to rob a drunken sailor, and would put all three into the street. They knew that the job would be done there, but they were not interested in the sailor; only in preserving the "good name" of the house."

The bouncers demonstrated their abilities the evening when Greenwood was present. A negro had his lips cut by one of the girls, precipitating a brawl based on ethnic origins. The four waiters moved in quickly and the offenders were ousted, with the waiters back serving within a few minutes.

80. Legless and soon to be wallet-less in the Ratcliffe Highway.

STRANGE SPORTS AND PASTIMES

Cock-fighting was one of the capital's most popular sports for hundreds of years, though some of the trainers of these fighting birds had somewhat unorthodox methods of preparation. Charles Cotton in 1675 advised:

> 'Towards four or five o'clock in the evening . . . having lick't their eyes and head with your tongue, put them in their pens and having filled their troughs with square-cut manchet, piss therein and let them feed while the urine is hot; for this will cause the scouring to work, and will wonderfully cleanse both head and body.'

Much has been written about cock-fighting and thankfully today the 'sport' has all but disappeared. Entertainment for the working population would take place mostly on a Sunday in the parks. After six days hard work the religious kill-joys would restrict the games allowed to the more tranquil like bowls and skittles, the only instrument allowed to be played being the organ. There was no shortage of 'fair' style entertainment. Accomplished horse-riding feats were extremely popular and you might see a man standing upright on horse-back riding around a course with a swarm of bees on his face. Across the way would be another entertainer riding two horses, with one foot on each, playing the flute. Another man would put on one of the most interesting shows which must have left the audience awestruck. He would pick up one hundred eggs each one a yard apart from its neighbour, all within a time-span of seventy-five minutes. Not to be missed!

For a small fee one could be fastened in the pillory and kissed by one of the girl attendants, although records do not show whether there was a choice!

Many Londoners had a great deal of imagination and precious little sense. The gatekeepers at the Halfpenny-hatch in Marylebone demanded a halfpenny entrance fee for the right to pass through private grounds shortening the journey to Primrose Hill. There was an added attraction to the walk as it was well known that one could see Edinburgh from this site. On Sunday evenings crowds of both sexes would meet, turn their backs on the city of London and look through their legs at the capital! The imagination was undoubtedly enhanced by the 'good sound ale brewed from good wholesome malt and hops' sold at fourpence the double mug. After a few of these, one could easily mistake one city for another, especially bent double looking between your own and maybe someone else's legs!

One of the biggest attractions in Stuart London was the fire-eater. A man named Richardson went to extraordinary lengths to cook his oyster. He would place a hot coal on his tongue and put the oyster on top. His assistant would heat the coal with bellows until the coal flamed and the oyster was ready for consumption. Not wishing to be wasteful Richardson would swallow both coal and oyster. When not cooking the entertainer might consume melted glass washed down with pitch and wax and sulphur, flambé of course, Richardson had an aversion to cold food.

Races, sometimes planned, others impromptu would take place in London's main streets. There were races for ladies in hooped petticoats and boys on donkeys. Many challenges were thrown out and the eating competition was one of the favourites. The most popular foods consumed were puddings and tripe. One man gambled that he and a friend could consume a bushel of tripe and four bottles of wine within one hour. There was no shortage of takers at £5 per head. The food and drink were laid out in the yard of a London tavern, and the man, without his friend, began the proceedings by eating a plate of tripe and drinking half a bottle of the wine. Those who had opposed him in the betting must have been mentally spending their winnings as there was no way he would consume the fare laid in front of him if he continued at such a slow rate. The tripe-eater then surprised everybody present as he poured the remaining three and a half bottles of wine over a vast heap of tripe. The entourage were still puzzling as to the man's tactics when a few minutes later their faces dropped. The gambler's friend was introduced and proceeded to demolish the remainder of the food. Bears have a voracious appetite.

THE GRINNING, WHISTLING AND YAWNING MATCHES

Although more common in the country areas, simple games were also played on the streets and in the ale-houses of the capital. Grinning matches, where contestants poked their head through a horse collar and smiled was one of the most basic of entertainments two hundred years ago. The slightly more educated might be found indulging in a whistling match, each contestant trying to continue their tune whilst trying to put off or outwhistle their opponents. In a smoking match either a large amount of tobacco or a small amount had to be consumed within a given period of time. The above entertainments probably gave rise to yet another — the yawning match — enough said!

Ferrets and tortoises might be raced, and ducks, hens and geese contributed to entertainment, usually in the form of gambling.

THE KISSING DANCE

In the early 1700s many dances were attacked by the church as being obscene. The 'Allemande' was particularly offensive to the self-appointed do-gooders as at one stage of the dance both man and woman roll on the floor, this leading to the exposure of the woman's legs. In another dance, appropriately named the 'kissing dance' the partners would join lips for several minutes at a time. It is not documented as to whether this was an 'excuse-me' or not.

RATS BOUGHT AND SOLD

There was no shortage of rats amongst the slums and sewers of mid-nineteenth century London and the capital's inhabitants, with their love of betting, soon devised a 'sport' which was to become popular amongst all classes. Bets were placed as to how many rats a dog could kill within a given period of time. The killings took place in large rat-pits whose proprietors would advertise 'Rats Wanted' and 'Rats Bought and Sold' and who would often keep up to two thousand rodents on the premises. Mayhew, amongst his travels in the under-world captures the details of the fights, as the expectant crowd around the ring await the 'entertainment:'

81. Ratting — the aim was to kill as many as possible within a given time period.

"the Captain preferred pulling the rats out of the cage himself, laying hold of them by their tails and jerking them into the arena. He was cautioned by one of the men not to let them bite him, for 'believe me' were the words 'you'll never forget Cap'an; these 'ere are none of the cleanest.' Whilst the rats were being counted out, some of those that had been taken from the cage ran about the panelled floor and climbed up the young officer's legs, making him shake them off and exclaim, 'Get out you varmint!'

'Chuck him in,' said the Captain, and over went the dog and in a second the rats were running round the circus, or trying to hide themselves between the small openings in the boards round the pit. Although the proprietor of the dog endeavoured to speak up for it, still it was evidently not worth much in a rat-killing sense; and if it had not been for its 'second' we doubt if the terrier would not have preferred leaving the rats to enjoy their lives . . .

Preparations now began for the grand match of the evening, in which fifty rats were to be killed. The dead 'uns were gathered up by their tails and flung into a corner. The floor was swept, and a big flat basket produced, like those in which chickens were brought to market, and under whose iron top could be seen small mounds of closely packed rats. This match seemed to be between the proprietor and his son, and the stake to be gained was only a bottle of lemonade. It was strange to observe the daring manner in which the lad introduced his hand into the rat cage as he fumbled about and stirred up with his fingers the living mass, picking up, as he had been requested 'only the big 'uns.'

When the fifty animals had been flung into the pit, they gathered themselves into a mound, which reached one-third up the sides. and which reminded one of a heap of hair-sweepings in a barber's shop after a heavy day's cuttings. These were all sewer and water-ditch rats, and the smell that rose from them was like that from a hot drain.

The Captain amused himself by flicking at them with his pocket handkerchief and offering them the lighted end of his cigar, which the little creatures tamely sniffed and drew back from, as they singed their noses. It was also a favourite amusement to blow on the mound of rats, for they seemed to dislike the cold wind, which sent them fluttering about like so many feathers; indeed whilst the match was going on whenever the little animals collected together forming a barricade as it were to the dog, the cry of 'Blow on 'em! blow on 'em!' was given by the spectators and the dog's second puffed at them as if extinguishing a fire . . .

When all the arrangements had been made the second and the dog jumped into the pit. The moment the terrier was loose he became quiet in a most business-like manner and rushed at the rats, burying his nose in the mound till he brought out one in his mouth. In a short time a dozen rats with wetted necks were lying bleeding on the floor, and the white paint of the pit became grained with blood. In a little time the terrier had a rat hanging to his nose which, despite his tossing, still held on. He dashed up against the sides, leaving a patch of blood as if a strawberry had been smashed there.

'Hi Butcher! hi, Butcher!' shouted the second, 'good dog, bur-r-r-h!' and he beat the sides of the pit like a drum, till the dog flew about with new life. 'Dead 'un! Drop it!' he cried when the terrier nosed a rat kicking on its side, as it slowly expired of its broken neck.

'Time!' said the proprietor, and the dog was caught up and held panting, his neck stretched out like a serpent's staring intently at the rats that still kept crawling about. The poor little wretches in the brief interval, as if forgetting their danger, again commenced cleaning themselves, some nibbling the ends of their tails, others hopping about, going now to the legs of the lad in the pit and sniffing at his trousers, or, strange to say, advancing smelling to within a few paces of their enemy the dog . . .

A plentiful shower of half-pence was thrown into the pit as a reward for the second.

A slight pause now took place in the proceedings, during which the landlord requested that the gentlemen 'would give their minds up to drinking. You know the love I have of you,' he added jocularly, 'and that I don't care for any of you;' whilst the waiter acompanied the invitation with a cry of 'Give your orders gentlemen,' and the lad with the rats (who incidentally lost the competition) asked if 'any gentlemen would like any rats?' "

A 'PETRIFIED WOMAN' AND 'THE LARGEST RAT ALIVE'

At the very end of the 'Victorian' era, Robert Machray and the illustrator Tom Browne determined to take in as much of the capital's night life as possible before the many changes they could see coming which would radically alter night-time entertainment forever. Their journeys were recorded in "The Night Side of London." Let's join them at an East-End menagerie:

"Your first impression of the menagerie is that it is one vast offensive smell. Having got somewhat accustomed to this odour, you go round with the crowd, and see a fine young lion in his cage, a couple of lionesses in a second, a black bear and a hyena in a third, half a dozen wolves in a fourth, some dejected-looking monkeys and a cat of the domestic variety in a fifth, a kangaroo in another, and so on. There are eight or ten cages in all, and certainly you can't in reason expect much more for twopence, which is the charge for admission.

On one side is an opening into a side-show, 'price one penny.' A man shouting on a box at the entrance to it, cries out in a loud voice that in the side-show are to be seen three of the 'greatest novelties in the whole world.' One of them, he tells you, is a petrified woman, the second is the smallest kangaroo in existence, and the third is the largest rat alive. A curious little collection, is it not? At any rate it draws an audience to the speaker on the box. In a minute or two he passes into the side-show and you will go with him. First he shows you the tiny kangaroo, a greyish-white, squirming creature, with long hind legs and a very long thick tail; it was born in the menagerie, the showman declares. Next, you are asked to gaze upon the petrified woman. You see a gruesome object in leathery brown skin. 'A little over a hundred years ago' says the showman in a solemn tone, 'this woman, a sister of mercy, was walking about just like you or me (We weren't walking about — but that's a detail.) She had gone with a rescue party into a mine in Wales, but she herself was lost. When her body was found years later in the mine, it was discovered in the petrified condition in which you now see it!' He invites any lady or gentleman in the audience to touch the Thing, but no one is in the least anxious to do so. Then he moves on to another box, pulls up a curtain, and discloses a handsome bright-eyed animal, the size of a fox, whch he assures you is the largest rat in the world; it was 'lately captured by a soldier in the Transvaal, and brought to this country; secured by us at enormous expense!'"

82. One of Tom Brown's excellent illustrations.

'WE SHALL FIGHT IN THE FIELDS AND IN THE STREETS'

Fighting ranged from a means of settling basic disputes in the street, to organised prize bare-knuckle bouts. Before the days of a regular police force everybody had to be able to defend themselves as best they could, though there is no doubt that some relished a good scrap more than others.

The Brief and Merry History of Great Britain describes the anarchy in the streets:

> "Combats are very common among the meaner sort of the people. The assailants begin with running up against each other, heads foremost, like rams, and afterwards come to boxing. Upon the beginning of any quarrel in the streets, the porters and dogs immediately run barking from all corners, and the handicrafts quit their garrets, and these together make a fair circle for the boxers. By the ancient custom of these combats, a man is not to strike his adversary on the ground, but must give him time to rise, and the standers-by take care to see these

laws strictly observed. They never part till one of them calls for quarter, which they seldom do till they are quite disabled. These exercises are in great esteem amongst the English, and not only diverting to the men, but to the women likewise. In the evenings of their sabbaths and festivals, 'tis common to see the streets filled with these sorts of rencounters; all kinds of servants being then at liberty, and generally well loaded with liquors, have frequent quarrels and bickerings about precedency. One may see mothers encourage their sons, and married women their husbands to engage, the latter holding their husbands' canes and children the meanwhile. And sometimes people of quality lay aside their wigs, swords and neckcloths to box, when they are insulted by mean persons, against whom they must not draw their swords, the rabble esteeming that to be the most rascally thing A Gentleman can be guilty of; for which reason a Lieutenant-General hath e'er now been seen with a swoln face and a black eye. A young Lord has made his name terrible to all the coachmen, carters and porters in London by his manual operations on their bodies, when their behaviour has been rude and insolent; he having often, as the phrase is, 'beaten them to mummy' for it."

Fights were not restricted to the male sex and with an eye to attracting a large crowd challenges were issued from one woman to another:

'I Elizabeth Wilkinson, of Clerkenwell, having had some words with Hannah Highfield, and requiring satisfaction, do invite her to meet me on the stage and box for three guineas, each woman holding half a crown in each hand, and the first woman that drops her money to lose the battle.'

The challenges were invariably accepted:

'I, Hannah Highfield, of Newgate Market, hearing of the resoluteness of Elizabeth Wilkinson, will not fail, God willing, to give her more blows than words, desiring home blows, and of her no favour.'

A BROKEN HEART

George Stevenson was the sort of man you wanted to count as a friend in the lawless days of highwaymen and footpads. An expert with both the quarterstaff and sword, he was famous amongst the men of Yorkshire for the terrifying weight of his punch; he was gossiped about by the womenfolk for another reason: George had the attractive face and sinewy physique of a Greek god.

Madame Thurleigh was young, attractive and married to a man twice her age who spent a great deal of time in the capital. As often happens with such a wide age difference one party or other becomes disenchanted and Madame Thurleigh was bored. She was much too young and wanton to sit at home chattering or sewing with her maids, she wanted action. With her husband away so often she determined to go to the ball alone. The head coachman was down with gout and would have to be replaced with his deputy. On a snowy winter's night in 1739 George Stevenson flicked the reins and the carriage headed off into the freezing night on a ten mile journey. Madame Thurleigh pulled her cloak tightly around her hoping its place might be taken by the burly Yorkshireman on the return journey.

This was to prove far more eventful than the outward voyage, as the words dreaded by all travellers emanated from the darkness.

We do not know whether the highwaymen finished their command of 'stand and deliver' as George's mind was as swift as his fists. The coachman drew his pistol and shot the first highwayman twice in quick succession. The other two steadied their horses in preparation for their attack and defying the bullets the Yorkshireman lashed out with his whip unseating both riders. The job was completed with George knocking out one of the attackers with the butt of his pistol and breaking another's jaw with a straight left.

George climbed into the carriage and comforted his mistress as she instructed him to do.

George was promoted and it was not long before he was into his master's shoes and his mistress's underwear. He literally wore the former when his master was away whilst she did not wear the latter in George's presence.

Indeed both parties were in a state of undress when Mr. Thurleigh unexpectedly burst into the bedroom. After drinking three bottles of port a day for years the rich businessman knew he was no physical match for the upstart of a coachman but vented his anger in a torrent of abuse and dismissed George on the spot. Madame Thurleigh managed to smuggle some money to her lover and they promised to write as soon as George established himself in London.

The coachman had little difficulty settling in the capital. He was admired by the men for his prowess in the ring and by the womenfolk from all backgrounds for his performance between the sheets. But as in all popular stories George could not and would not forget his first love, the lady whose life he had saved in the woods. Why hadn't she contacted him? The weeks turned to months and as George skipped and trained and honed his magnificent physique he knew he would have to do something drastic if he were ever to see her again.

The champion pugilist of the time was the fearsome Jack Broughton who was so confident of his ability that he issued a challenge in "The Flying Post" on the 1st January, 1741. He invited all-comers to take him on for the championship of England, opponents having three months in which to issue their challenge. Such was Jack's reputation that with the three months drawing to a close not one man dare challenge him. Just before the deadline the champion received the following communication:

"Mr. Broughton,

You think yourself a great fighter. Perhaps you are; but there's people living in Clerkenwell say your fighting days are over and are good for nothing but to show off at them fights. I will meet you a month from today. If you don't come up you are a coward. If you don't dust me you are a humbug. If I beat you, you are a dead man."

Today's promoters could not have improved upon the promotion of the fight. George had left his challenge late to gain the maximum publicity in the hope that the news would travel the two hundred miles to Yorkshire and tempt his ex-lover to witness the fight and maybe reunite after the contest. He had one small obstacle to overcome first however, the boxing champion of England, Jack Broughton.

83. Did he break George Stevenson's heart?

A thunderous cheer went up as George jumped into the ring. The crowd had tired of the wrestling and fencing exhibitions and were screaming for the fight to begin. With princes being fanned by their lady friends in the gallery and children sitting expectantly on their father's shoulders George surveyed the scene. He was only looking for one person. Had she come? George paid scant attention to the captain of the fight's instructions, he could not spot her amongst the vast crowd.

The first round is fairly even. The champion has the advantage in height and reach but Stevenson is stockier and faster. George bloodies the champion's nose in round two which is terminated when Broughton is forced to the ground. The crowd has seen nothing so brutal for years as the champion's eyes swell and the challenger's ribs receive sledgehammer blows. The coachman has noticed somebody in the gallery and he momentarily drops his guard. His teeth are knocked out with one punch as he loses interest in the fight. He has seen somebody he knows in the gallery, somebody he has not seen for a long time. She has come. He also sees somebody he has never seen before. A young cavalier is stroking her cheek, they are whispering as lovers do, giving more attention to each other than to the fight. His gesture has been in vain. With no further interest in the fight George staggers around the ring. The champion seizes his chance to finish the contest and musters all his strength for a punch just below the now broken heart.

He lies unconscious with the concerned champion saying he will never box again. George Stevenson dies within a month though who did the greater damage to his heart we can only guess.

CANNABIS: *'of considerable use for lunatics'*

Any Sherlock Holmes devotee could be forgiven for believing that behind the doors of gentlemen in the capital, many were 'shooting up' on cocaine — 'the seven per cent solution.' Nothing could be further from the truth. Some doctors and researchers experimented with coca leaves, following the example of the South Americans and chewing the leaves, expecting the drug to give them energy and dispense with the need for sustenance over a fairly long period of time. An American walker named Weston experimented with the leaves in the capital in 1876, he finding them of no use to his favourite hobby and even condemning them as acting as a kind of opiate.

Coca was used to make wine, and in the treatment of gout with coca sherry and port also being marketed. Some doctors argued that it was a cure for shyness:

> 'It causes timid people who are usually ill at ease in society . . . to appear to good advantage.'

It was not until the leaves were treated that its possible use as an anaesthetic was discussed and the drug became of interest to those wishing to act as guinea pigs in the cause of science or pursuit of new pleasures. Cocaine was not to become a problem until long after the Victorian age had passed.

Cannabis or Indian hemp was introduced to London centuries before coca leaves and it was seen to be something 'to put a man into a dream' and therefore 'be of considerable use for lunatics'. In nineteenth century London, after a report from a Dr. William O'Shaughnessy, cannabis resin was converted into extract and tincture and considered a respectable drug, even though O'Shaughnessy had commented on 'the strange balancing gait and perpetual giggling' of those under the influence. A cannabis 'farm' was even set up near Mitcham for commercial cultivation.

Because of the unreliability of supply, cannabis was not often prescribed by doctors and the debate as to whether it caused or cured insanity lasted throughout the century. A few romantics and rebels might be found in the Cheshire Cheese in the Strand towards the end of the century, but all in all 'bang' was not considered dangerous or addictive, and was paid scant attention by the vast majority of Londoners.

'THE FOOD SCARCE FIT FOR HOGS' LIFE IN THE WORKHOUSE

Workhouses were institutions where when you have to go there they have to let you in. They were a kind of 'safety net' for the very poor, elderly or very young who had absolutely nowhere else to go. Although many millions preferred life on the street, it was the last home for many tens of thousands.

In the first half of the nineteenth century conditions were extremely harsh. Married couples would be separated and even mothers from their babies and children, this being all the more harsh as many admitted were one-parent families. In the St. Marylebone workhouse premature weaning was enforced, the reasoning behind these strict rules being that children should not be corrupted by mixing with adult paupers.

84. Marylebone Workhouse. The writing was on the wall.

Elaborate laws were devised to punish those who contravened the workhouse rules. Being dirty, refusing to work and swearing were amongst the most common offences and punishments varied between having to wear certain clothes for two days to appearing before a magistrate and being flogged or confined in punishment rooms. Paupers were expected to remain silent at mealtimes and had little control over any visitors they might receive.

Upon admission to a workhouse the paupers' clothes would be taken away, fumigated and kept until the day of departure. They would then be bathed, and disinfected, the men not being allowed razors, shaving and bathing being allowed only once a week. The uniforms were ill-fitting, and both sexes were given the same standard hair-cut. Beds were very close together and there were no lockers for personal possessions as it was feared that pieces of food might be hoarded.

Once in the workhouse it was extremely difficult to get out as the work was not paid, but just went to the maintenance of the institution. It was therefore impossible to save. Much of the work was similar to that carried out by convicts, stone-breaking and oakum-picking being amongst the more common tasks.

The food was often worse than that inflicted upon prisoners. Bread with either cheese or gruel was the staple diet, being supplemented by meat, suet pudding or potatoes anything up to three times a week. Much of the food was served cold as inmates were forced to line up and march into the dining area. Sometimes the cooks were of a very low standard, and the wardens did not allocate all the supplies delivered. There was a further risk of the food being contaminated. Of 57 samples of milk tested at one London workhouse nearly all were diluted with water, with seven being half-water, half-milk. Bosh butter was a serious risk to health as a combination of animal and horse fat or other substances was often passed off as butter.

Despite the fact that many of the inmates were illiterate, letters of complaint were delivered to the governing authorities. The following letter was delivered to Somerset House in 1843:

"Gentlemen, Do for Gods sake take into consideration the sufferings of the poor of Lambeth Work-house ill used and half starved — the master a perfect brute swearing at sick and aged driving them to Work when scarce able to stand — some of you I know to be men of feeling — my information I know is correct   yours respectfully,
A. Parishoner

P.S. The food scarce fit for Hogs.

84a-d. Poplar Workhouse 1908-11. (Tower Hamlets Library).

84b.

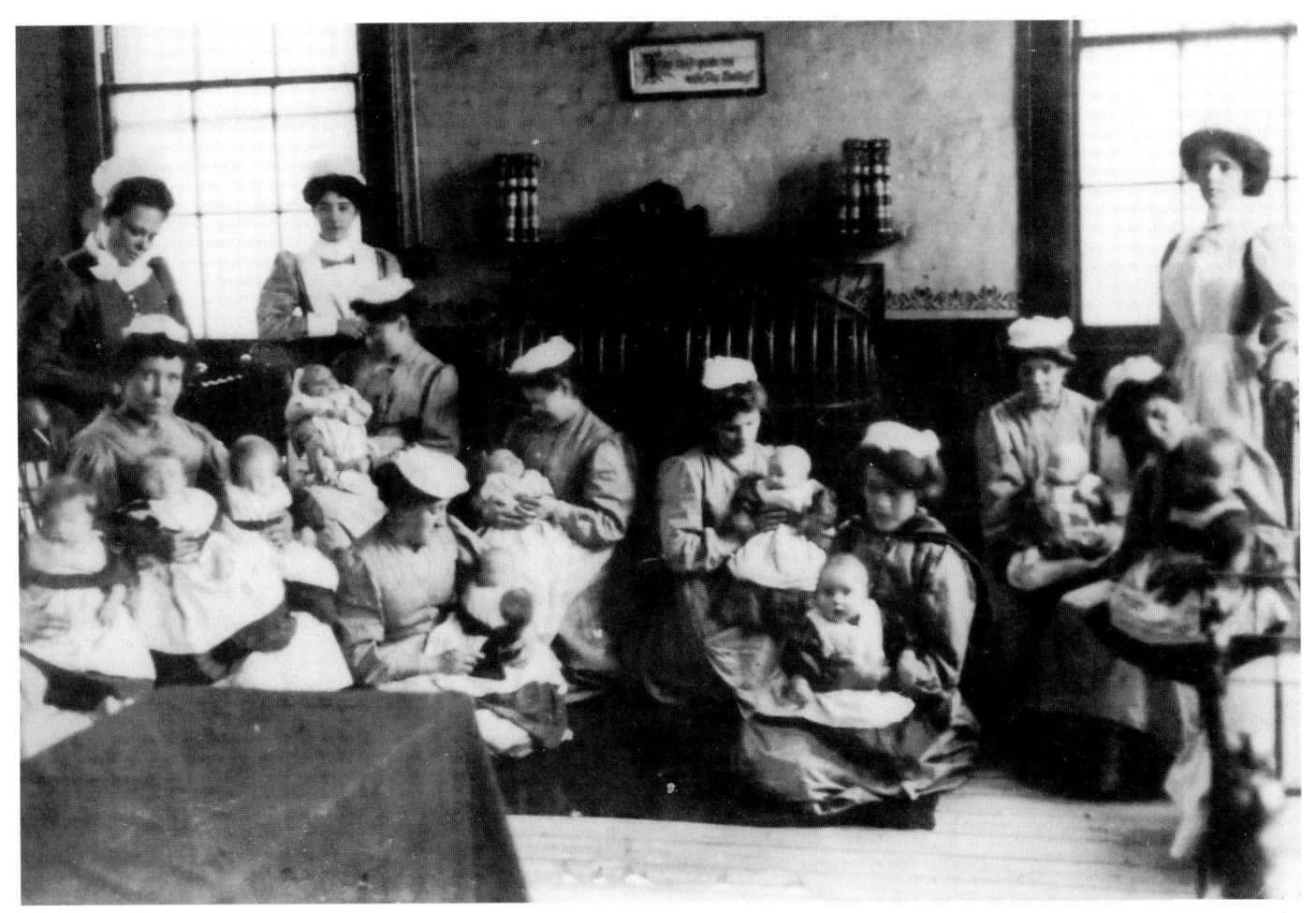

84c.

84d.

85. Men's hostel towards the end of the nineteenth century.

86. Dinner Time in the St. Pancras Workhouse.

'LAST SCENE OF ALL'

SUICIDE IN VICTORIAN LONDON

87. Life and death.

Many preferred a complete end to their lives rather than experience the atrocious conditions the poor had to endure. As we started our journey through London with the premature birth of a baby on the streets, it would seem apt to finish with a brief examination of premature death, or suicide, in the capital.

"A merry Christmas and a happy new year." Charlie shouted the greetings to anyone who might have been listening in Waterloo the first day of 1861. The greetings and apparent cheerfulness had been induced by the alcohol he had consumed. Though usually a fairly moderate drinker for the times, the 53 year old millwright consumed 'a little drop' according to his son-in-law and was just beginning to sober up in the early hours of the morning. Charlie Sudds had fallen on hard times, being laid off after twenty-five years service, in order that a cheaper man could be employed. He could certainly have had no great expectations as to the future as in the winter of 1861 business was very bad, the days short and frost had closed the Thames. In the early hours of 1861 Charlie Sudds shot himself in the kitchen.

In the same year a 55 year old man who was worried about having an operation for 'a stoppage in his water' threw himself from an upstairs window.

James Jeffries was a particularly sensitive employee working as a chemist's porter. When he heard of a complaint about himself he announced 'It's all over with me now' and took his last drink — prussic acid.

Most London suicides could be attributable to one or more of the following problems; illness, drink, business problems, public disgrace or family and emotional problems. In Victorian London three times as many men as women were likely to commit suicide. Those in the 35-55 age range were most at risk, with poison being the most favoured method. The number of deaths through drowning in the Thames is not nearly as high as might be suspected from reading the literature and examining the illustrations of the times. Those who did jump were usually servant girls who appeared to prefer Blackfriars Bridge to London Bridge. Many of them just climbing down and easing themselves into the water, not wanting to make a splash, they would just float quietly away.

It is through examining true stories rather than a mass of statistics that we can gain a realistic image of how life and death must have been looked upon over one hundred years ago. The following stories all took place between 1860-1870.

James Mason was described by his betting agent as being 'very excited, very nervous and very reserved.' The last observation may have resulted from the forty-five year old's job as valet to Lord Ashburton. Upon reading a letter delivered to him by his employer's groom the valet 'rushed upstairs very fast indeed, without a candle.' The door to his room was found to be locked the next morning, and when he still hadn't emerged by late afternoon, a locksmith, a carpenter and a policeman were called in, all three to be confronted with a sight they would never forget. Dressed in only his day shirt James Mason was found hanging by a scarf from the bedpost. The letter he had received the previous night was nowhere to be found and his gold watch was missing. What the authorities did find gave some clues to the valet's behaviour. There was a letter to his brother stating that he would probably be dismissed (due to his increasing consumption of alcohol) and some evidence that James had been a gambling man.

Despite the fact that he was to be sacked this did not necessarily mean the workhouse for the valet as for four years previously he had been granted an annuity of £20. Mason was described by his employer's surgeon as being 'a peculiar silent man' and largely as a result of this 'evidence' the jury returned a verdict of temporary insanity.

About a year later in Maida Vale two policemen were forcing open another door, locked — all be it temporarily, against the cruel outside world. The method of Emma Austin's suicide was not as dramatic as that of James Mason but equally as effective. A local doctor was sent for and one did not need to be highly qualified to determine the cause of death, a bottle of laudanum being on prominent display in the room. At 42 Emma was living apart from her husband and working as a laundress. When her husband refused to give her money for the rent, he objecting to her continued drunkenness, Emma made the second, and successful attempt on her life. The case is interesting for the views expressed after Emma's death. Because she wrote 'a quantity of poetry' dedicated to her husband she was considered to be of a romantic persuasion, and therefore likely to be of unsound mind. The scientific evidence provided by Dr. Beale after a post-mortem advocated 'that the state of the brain indicated unsoundness of mind'!

MELANCHOLY SUICIDE OF A LADY AT ISLEWORTH FERRY.

88. Both sexes used poison, men also employed sharp instruments and women took to the water.

The poetry found on the mantlepiece would suggest a broken heart rather than a diseased brain.
From Emma to her husband Harry;

> The treasure I have had and lost,
> Oh, could I but regain,
> Not for all the wealth the world might cost,
> I would not act the same.
>
> My Harry to my arms once more,
> Oh, could I have you again,
> Then to my God I would implore,
> For happiness to remain.
>
> Oh Harry! is your heart so hard
> That it can no more relent
> To the prayer of your penitent
> When she says she does repent?

George Dewing was bankrupt. His physical health was generally sound apart from a little bronchitis. He had a very low self-esteem and felt that he had let his wife down, but still not forty years old he decided to end his life by taking cyanide of potassium.

'Good bye my dear little wife, I hope you will soon get a kind and more prosperous if not independent husband you are worthy of.' Thus opened the last letter George ever wrote finishing the tear-stained communication some two pages later 'farewell farewell George.' The printer's despair may be witnessed by excerpts from his suicide note;

'Good bye my mother thou paragon of virtue loving kindness and untiring industry God bless you. Good bye my dear sisters Betsey Mary Jane who are ever kind. Poor Jane (a woman of intelligence industry and domestic economy) I hope she will soon be relieved from her misery and poverty and drunken sot of a husband. I tried every move but without success to put myself beyond debt and difficulty and live in independency with the world but you have only to be branded with the name of Dewing and its the guinea stamp to be poor and in difficulties however vigilant, perservering industrious and economising you may be. My father grandfathers uncles aunts sisters brother cousins &c that bear the fated name I hope I leave no offspring behind to inherit it, to be looked upon coldly by the world to be shunned and frowned at by acquaintance and treated with a contumely and contempt by those you love and respect all because you are poor and fates against you.

Poison was employed by both sexes, there were differences however as to other methods used. Many women would drown themselves, be it in the canal or in the Serpentine where a special patrol was set up. Men favoured sharp instruments such as knives or razors. Most suicides were rather humdrum affairs and if there was not a whiff of scandal or some exotic means of doing away with one's life, the news rarely warranted more than a few lines in the local newspaper. Victorians often joked a great deal about suicide attempts, especially women who would throw themselves into the river only when they heard a policeman coming.

The Monument was the scene of six well-published suicide leaps between 1788-1842. An iron cage painted white was erected at the top much to the amusement of foreign visitors. The would-be suicide moved on to Highgate Archway where later in the nineteenth century four 'successful' leaps were made in as many months before the architecture was altered and a policeman employed to patrol the area.

A famous piece of nonsense verse handed down from generation to generation in slightly varying forms made light of the question of suicide, an option still only employed as a last resort by a very small number of Londoners.

> 'There was a man in his garden walked
> And cut his throat with a lump of chalk,
> His wife, she knew not what she did,
> She strangled herself with the saucepan lid.
> There was a man and a fine young fellow
> Who poisoned himself with an umbrella.
> Every Joey in his cradle
> Shot himself with a silver ladle.'

> **'Guns aren't lawful;**
> **Nooses give;**
> **Gas smells awful;**
> **You might as well live'**

89. Better luck next time.

Tragical History Tours Ltd.

PRESENT

TRIP TO MURDER

A unique three hour evening bus trip combining cultural with criminal, history with horror. Jack the Ripper, a haunted house, Greenwich, Tower, two pub stops, live commentary.

EVERY EVENING EXCEPT MONDAY

Reservations for all trips Tel: (0181) 857 1545.
Prices: Adults £15.50; Students £12.50; Children £10.50
includes Fish & Chip Supper.
Live expert commentary on all tours.

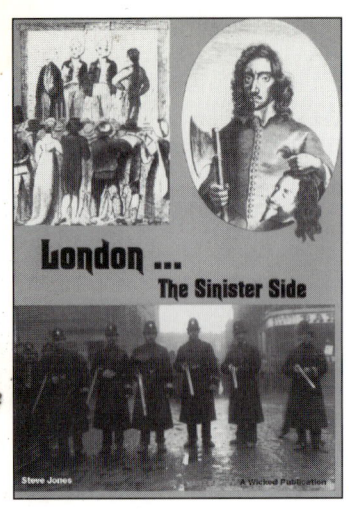

(1) London… The Sinister Side

Reprinted every year since 1986. Includes chapters on Jack the Ripper, The Kray Twins, executions, the hangmen of London, prisons. If you are interested in the darker side of London's history, its ghosts, murderers, mystery and misery, then join us in our trip through London… The Sinister Side.

(2) Wicked London

Murder 'Orrible Murder, the Blitz, early operations and the darker side of everyday life.

(4) Capital Punishments

These wicked tales of yesteryear are centred around crime, domestic violence and prison conditions in Victorian London. Including sections on juvenile crime, dangerous women, the lighter side of court life and women in prison.

(5) In Darkest London

Prostitutes, criminals, backstreet abortionists, strikers and the police give lengthy accounts of their activities in a frank and unsentimental look at London life from the death of Victoria to the outbreak of the Second World War.

(6) When the Lights Went Down

Many took the opportunities presented by the War to help themselves rather than their country. Murderers, black-marketers, prison-officers and ARP workers talk about their war.

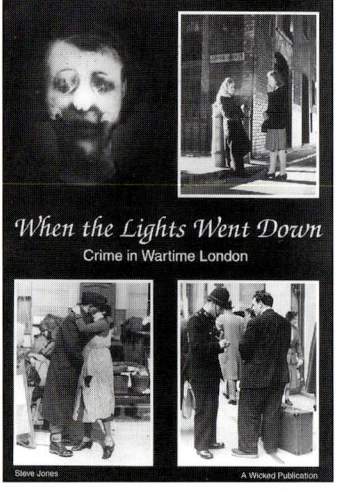

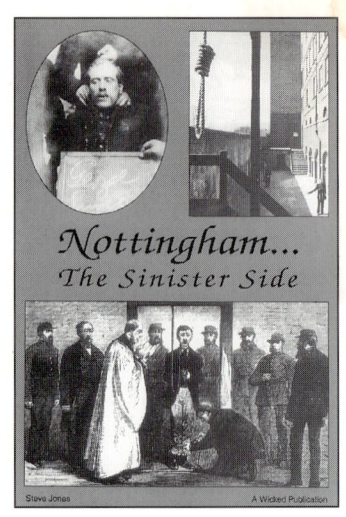

(7) Nottingham… The Sinister Side

Although internationally famous for being the home of Britain's most famous outlaw, Robin Hood, Nottingham, like all large cities, has housed tens of thousands of lawbreakers with no intention whatsoever of giving to the poor.

The most famous murderers include 'Nurse' Waddingham who poisoned two of her patients for their inheritance, and Herbert Mills, who executed 'the perfect murder' in order to sell his story to the newspapers – both were hanged.

(8) Manchester … The Sinister Side

With the presence of over 100 photographs and illustrations, join us in a trip back in time to meet the incorrigible rogues, vagabonds and thieves in Victorian Manchester and the atrocious conditions endured by the vast majority of the population.

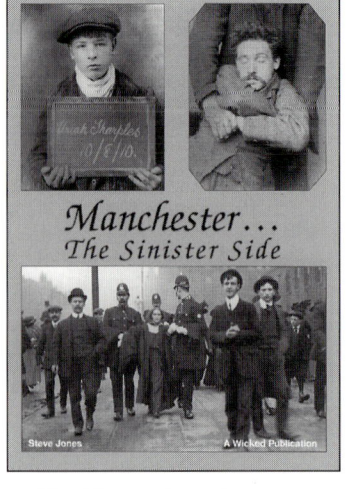

All books are A4 with approximately 80 photographs/illustrations to supplement the wicked tales of yesteryear.

Wicked Publications, 222 Highbury Road, Bulwell, Nottingham NG6 9FE
Telephone: Nottingham (0115) 975 6828 or London (0181) 311 3888